Note to Self: EMPOWERMENT

7 Steps to Help You Find Your True Self, Purpose, and Power Within

Trina Hall

Copyright © 2016 Trina Hall

All rights reserved.

ISBN: 0995216800
ISBN-13: 978-0-9952168-0-8

DEDICATION

To my beautiful daughters, Jasmine and Brooklyn. You girls are my life and mean the world to me. We stuck together and our special bond will forever be unbreakable.

To my husband Jason. You are the love of my life and my biggest supporter. Thank you for loving me and my girls unconditionally.

CONTENTS

	ACKNOWLEDGMENTS	i
1	SUFFERING SILENTLY	1
2	WHO AM I?	18
3	STEP 1: DISCOVER YOUR TRUTH	33
4	STEP 2: TRUST YOURSELF	55
5	STEP 3: REMOVE TOXIC PEOPLE	84
6	STEP 4: SAY NO	101
7	STEP 5: THINK POSITIVE AND SHOW GRATITUDE	119
8	STEP 6: FORGIVE AND TAKE YOUR POWER BACK	139
9	STEP 7: LIVE IN THE MOMENT	153
10	YOU GOT THIS!	170

ACKNOWLEDGMENTS

I could probably fill up an entire book with all of the names of people whom I would like to thank. I know that it is impossible to acknowledge everyone personally, but I will do my best to cover you all collectively.

Thank you Dr. Wayne Dyer. I only heard about you two weeks prior to meeting you at the *Writing From Your Soul* event in Fort Lauderdale, Florida. You took the time to connect with my daughter, Jasmine and I, even though we were holding up the huge line of people who have followed you for several years. I instantly felt a spiritual connection with you that still inspires me to this day. Words cannot describe the impact you have made on my life, along with countless others across the globe.

A heartfelt thanks to Roger Love. You have helped me to find my voice, so that I am able to use it to inspire and help others. Your genuine, kind heart has strengthened the belief in myself to pursue my purpose. Your words of encouragement have been a force behind writing this book.

Thank you Brendon Burchard for your inspiration and motivation.

To my soul family in the Hay House Community. You have been an important part of this journey. My love and gratitude for each and every one of you is eternal.

Extra special thanks to Lisa, Kevin, Abby and Liam Johnson, Ron and Toni Stewart, Kim and Hovic Bagh, Mandy

Lawrence, Angie Hewitt and Mark Carvalho for being there during my lowest days.

Many thanks to Jason Pake for designing my amazing book cover. I am also extremely grateful for my editor, Jasmine Stewart and my videographer, Brooklyn Koeslag.

Thank you Don and Chris Folliott for always believing in me. Your continuous support, love and encouragement is greatly appreciated.

Thank you to my writing accountability buddy, Kim Louise Morrison, who has been a tremendous support. You have become a dear friend and have played a key role throughout this entire process. Thank you George Carroll for matching us up and leading the way.

I could never forget to thank: Tara Bostock, Renee Smith, Colleen Campbell, Ron Campbell, Tamiah Johnston, Tammie Hall, Heather Besley, Amie Adams, Ann Gooda, Sharon Fonger, Stephanie Tran, Sonia Imertl, Jordan Fitzgerald, Ken Pernu, and Michelle Schaefle. You all hold a special place in my heart. So do Christina, Alina, Summer, Mark, Jacob and Julian.

Most importantly, a warm thanks to you, the reader of this book. Also to everyone who follows my blogs, shares my quotes, and has been incredibly supportive throughout this journey. There are too many of you to mention and I do not want to leave anyone out. You know who you are.

xoxoxo

1

SUFFERING SILENTLY

On the outside, my world always looked perfect. Little did anyone know that I was suffering silently. No matter how hard I tried, I never felt like I was good enough. I tried my hardest to embody all of the characteristics that would cause the least amount of resistance and conflict. I did not want to upset anyone, or get them angry. I created a life built from everyone else's desires and expectations of me. I would meet each impossible demand, only to be "thanked" with more of them. I got so caught up in pleasing everyone else that I became completely detached from my true self. I never thought that I would find my way back, since I never knew who I truly was in the first place.

    I became the master of masking my low self-esteem. I have been put down, knocked down and kicked repeatedly while I was down. I would always get back up, but never long enough to gain full force. Deep down, I knew that there was more to my life. There was always a part of me that would shine brightly from within, even during my darkest days. Others clearly recognized this in me and would try to dim my light. They tried to keep me playing small, although inside my dreams were huge. I understood the psychology of a bully. If I showed weakness, I would be preyed upon even more. I continued to keep my head held high. Many times it took every ounce of strength I had.

I stayed positive and optimistic, even when life showed me no mercy. Too many people depended on me. No one had any clue that my entire life was completely falling apart. Not even my closest friends were aware of my chronic stress. My world came crashing down, and somehow I had to figure out a way to put myself back together. While doing so, I learned many valuable lessons, which I am going to share with you.

This is my first book and I want it to be perfect. I have been through numerous struggles in life. Many people have one major event or story, which they use to teach others what they have learned - I have countless. I find this challenging when writing because I have several books in me. I feel this one is a great start. Having people find their true selves and having them live an authentic fulfilling life is the key, as it creates a solid foundation to build upon. Every other aspect of your life will fall into place, if we get this right first.

I want to help as many people as possible. In order to do so, I am going to have to be vulnerable and will open up about many of my poor choices. Without these tough lessons, I would not have the tools to help you. I have also realized that no matter what I say or do, I will never be able to please certain people. I may as well just be myself and do the best I can. Hopefully, the ego will be brushed aside, so a greater spiritual lesson can be learned.

Dr. Wayne Dyer, would often quote Pierre Teilhard de Chardin, *"We are not human beings having a spiritual experience. We are spiritual beings having a human experience."* With that perspective, life merely is a series of learning events. It is not the human being who is hurting us, rather it is a soul embodied in human form, trying to teach us a spiritual lesson. Because I have a deep understanding of this, I have no grudges against anyone. I no longer have any emotional attachment, pain or ill feelings toward those whom have hurt me. However, it did take me some time to get to this point. People do the best they can, at whatever level they are at.

This book is not intended to hurt anyone or destroy their reputation. I have been hesitant and careful while writing this book. I have tried to find a way to not mention a few people, but there was absolutely no way around it. They have been my greatest teachers. It is being written with only the purest intentions to help and to serve you. You are my main focus. If I help one more person, it is worth putting this book out there. I will not risk missing out on saving someone. Maybe that one person is you, or someone close to you?

That means I cannot sit back and say nothing, while I keep the many lessons that I have learned to myself. I have spent most of my life keeping things inside. It has only been in the past couple of years that I have started to share some of my story on the internet and to the world. I learned that the more I opened up about myself, the more I helped people. It is more effective to teach wisdom with a story associated with it. Therefore, I will tactfully and truthfully reveal only what is necessary, in order to pass along some of my insights to you. I will also change a few names and have some remain nameless for privacy.

I have put a lot of pressure on myself, so please be gentle on me. I have taken courses, read many books, and have traveled to attend seminars researching my topic by learning from the top leaders of this industry. But nothing beats the four decades of wisdom and incredible life experience I have gained. I have been through enough struggles to know what works and what does not. I feel I have an important message, as we all do.

Life seems to be moving at hyper speed. We get busy with work, family, friends, pets...the list is endless - not to mention all of the extracurricular activities. If you have children, you know how it is like. You are constantly running around after them. You are driving them to school, to their lessons, their games, the mall and their friend's house. How do you balance your job, your kids *and* a relationship? When do you have time for yourself? You spend your entire days meeting the demands of others and you ignore your own issues. You are exhausted and want to relax, so you go on the internet, watch television or just plain pass out. You feel like it is no big deal that your own issues are being pushed aside. You go to sleep, only to wake up and relive a similar day to the one before.

NOTE TO SELF: EMPOWERMENT

There are too many external distractions telling us how to act, when the answers are inside of you. The problem is that our lives are too full to figure out our true selves. How do you really think? What do you really want? What do you like or dislike? These seem like simple questions, but you would be amazed at the number of people who do not really know the answers.

How could you know? Life is too demanding and fast-paced. You do not want to be a pain and bother anyone with *your* problems. With the internet and texting being the primary way we communicate, talking on the phone or in person is becoming a thing of the past. Our minds are too overwhelmed, with very little release. You want to be positive and be happy. You want to show strength, so you keep your worries inside. Your seemingly small problems will compile, compound, and escalate if they are not dealt with right away. We cannot afford to take the time to heal. As soon as we can manage and are able to pretend like nothing is wrong, we go back at it again. Many of us have not even dealt with our childhood issues. As adults, many of us grow up with the wounded child within us - unhealed and unrevealed. We fool ourselves when things look great on the outside.

Does this sound like you? Are you feeling as if your own needs are being ignored? Like you are always there for everyone else, and no one does the same for you? Maybe you have become accustomed to it? Maybe you are unsure of your own needs? I am here to force you to pay attention to yourself. **You matter.** Your needs are just as important. If you continue to give, with nothing in *return, you may start to have resentment. If you do not address your pain, it will continue to grow deep inside you. You can be optimistic all you want, but it does not change the fact that your unresolved issues are still there. I care about you enough to tell you the hard truth. The truth shall set you free.* I will help you resolve your concerns, with less pain and in less time. It will hurt way more if you drag this out. The time is now! I know it can be difficult at first to face your situations, but I do not want you to suffer any longer than you have to. You deserve to be happy.

I see where many people are heading and it is not good. I will not sit back without a fight. I am on a mission to prevent this from happening to you.

OUR CULTURE IS FOCUSING TOO MUCH ON OUTWARD APPEARANCES

People are too busy and would rather avoid dealing with the pain. They are in denial. People are wanting the fastest and easiest fix. Denial, drugs and alcohol are merely a temporary coping mechanism. The pain is masked, but in reality it is compiling underneath the surface. This way is proven not to work, yet people continue to turn to these methods of dealing with their problems. They are not ready to face their harsh reality. Some people are not aware that they even have problems.

That is why you see many celebrities in the media struggling. They have money and fame, but they are not happy. Their dreams have been reached and often surpassed, yet they sabotage it all. They may turn to drugs and alcohol, or they become workaholics. They focus on anything else, so they do not have to deal with what is *really* going on inside of them. We are no different.

WE ARE BORN WITH A PURPOSE

We are all born a perfect, innocent miracle, with the necessary power within us. We know we are born for a reason and have a purpose, but what is it? Why is it so hard to figure out? People are getting more and more disconnected from who they truly are. Somehow we got lost and damaged. *Your job is to peel away all the layers of hurt, betrayal, guilt, and regrets until you return back to the greatness which is inside of you.*

When you are out of touch with your true self, you make decisions based on what others want and expect. You feel you need to give an answer quickly and do not give yourself the time to really think about it. Your life turns to autopilot, until eventually you get to a place in your life and wonder how you even got there? Before you know it, you may have regrets.

Are you surrounded by negative and controlling people who do not have your best interests at heart? Are some of these people your family and close friends? They can make it difficult for you to try and break free. Your heart is involved when they are people you love, or ones who are supposed to love you. They take advantage of your good nature, by pouring on the guilt and using manipulation as a control tactic. You may be a heart-centered person and your heart takes control of all the decisions you make. You may be criticized and put down. It can be exhausting when defending yourself against these people. You might choose to stay quiet in order to avoid confrontation. It seems easier to just give up and give in. They are often demanding and monopolize your time, so you cannot think clearly for yourself. These people are generally not accepting of your desire to change. They do not want to lose control of you. You may realize that the closest people to you are the ones who are hurting you the most.

Have you lost yourself? Are you not having enough "me" time? Is your life revolving around everyone else? Are you constantly trying to save people and are tired of all the drama? Do you keep trying to improve other people's lives, then somehow find yourself depleted and having to build yourself back up?

People are living unfulfilled lives. They are working in jobs they are not happy with, and are making just enough to pay the bills. There is no passion or purpose because they are doing what is expected of them, while playing different roles and wearing different masks. They are living their lives for others and are people pleasers. They do not even know who they are anymore. You also may not know, because people are always trying to tell you how to be. There are so many demands and you are getting pulled in all different directions. We are getting bogged down with too many things all at once. Society is turning to social media and watching reality shows. All this is dealing with other people's lives and is distracting you from your own. We are disconnecting from ourselves way too easily. Things need to change, and the sooner the better.

The good news is that you *can* change this. If you are not happy with any part of your life, you can take control of any situation and switch it around entirely. I am here to help you, before you reach rock bottom like I did.

PEOPLE ARE WAKING UP

The world is shifting. People are waking up to the truth and they are becoming more aware. They are craving something more for their lives. They are frustrated with their old ways and are gaining more strength. People are tired of pleasing and trying to keep up with impossible expectations. They are tired of being lied to, taken advantage of, taken for granted, and being played the fool.

We are starting to stand up for ourselves. We are using our voices, when we once stayed quiet. We cannot take it anymore. We are becoming intolerant of negative people and bullies who continually drag us down. We have had enough of our family members, friends, bosses, co-workers, and partners treating us like crap. All the insults, guilt, and manipulation are no longer working. Do you feel like there is more to your life? There definitely is better out there for you...and you deserve it.

YOU CAN DO THIS

If you are reading this book, you are wanting a change. You have the desire to improve your quality of life. Whatever stage you are at in life, there is always room for growth. There is always the next level. You may feel like you are in too big of a mess, and it is impossible to get out of it. I am here to tell you that you can. If you are unable to think straight, I will help you to get rid of all the clutter and provide you with a clear mindset. I understand that you may have been hurt too many times and do not know who to trust. I can assure you that I am looking out for your well-being and I am only here to help you. It is up to you, if you want to receive the help and use the tools I will provide you.

I am hoping to connect with you on a deep level. I want to make a positive difference in your life, like I have with many others around the world. Each person I help matters. **You matter to me.** There is no greater reward than making a positive impact on another's life. I love being a part of someone's transformation. The joy and light that shines in their eyes as they express gratitude, is what I live for.

I have spent most of my life fixing others, but neglected to help myself. The Universe forced me to find my true self when my entire world came crashing down. I honestly thought I had surpassed my limit of Inner strength, as I have been counting on it my entire life. I went from having everything on the outside, to losing everything...including my identity. In the process, I have learned many valuable lessons that I want to share with you. I was stripped away of my entire life, but was left with a shred of inner strength, which I cannot believe carried me through. I have built my life from the inside out. So if you even have an ounce of inner strength, I have high hopes for you. If I could do it, so can you.

I have learned the hard way, and the lessons from these challenges are instilled in me. I have been through many highs and lows in life. I was great at giving advice, but rarely took any of it myself. I used to always put myself last. Then I realized I was doing it all wrong, so I mastered this new approach. Since using my process, I feel strong enough to carry the weight of the world. I have done all the inner work. I am sure of who I am. I have an endless supply of personal power that enables me to help people each day, without feeling depleted. I have found my voice, purpose and power. I have shared some of these steps in my blog, life coaching and my seminar, with incredible results.

After you learn my process, your life will never be the same and you will not look back. I later found out that some of my findings are similar to the wisdom of Oprah, Dr. Wayne Dyer and Tony Robbins, which is a great validation to me that I am on the right track. But these are my own unique stories and process. If you follow my steps, it will help you take control of your own life. It will also lead you along the same path to finding your true self, purpose and power from within.

My life is better than I could ever imagine and it keeps soaring to new levels. I would have never believed it if you told me when I was alone in my room, depressed and destitute - when ending my life seemed like the only viable solution. I am living proof that my process works. I turned my entire life around and got rid of all the drama. I finally found the man of my dreams, who treats me better than I could have ever imagined. Jay and I get to travel and enjoy life together. My two daughters, Jasmine and Brooklyn, are both thriving. I have a life filled with love and peace. I now do what I love for work and stay true to my purpose. I have more freedom and time to do whatever I chose, with the ones I love. I live each day with ease, as my life continues to flow.

I finally realized what truly matters in life. I will share this with you in hopes to help you find your true self, purpose, and your power within. When you find this, your life will be fulfilling and you will become unstoppable. The possibilities are endless.

It is time to take control of your life. I will retell my journey every step of the way. I will guide you through the process so you are not alone. There is no worse feeling than feeling like you are going through a difficult time by yourself. I will not allow you to feel that way. I am here to motivate and uplift you. I will assist you with creating a solid foundation of unwavering strength. We will uncover who you truly are and what you really want.

IT IS POSSIBLE

The reality is that we are in charge of our own lives and we all have choices. You can change anything in your life that you are not happy with. You do not have to accept things as they are, or tolerate people mistreating you. It is natural to become more tolerant of people treating us poorly when they are family members. We need to become accountable and no longer be the victim.

Clearly some things have not been working for you and that is why you are looking to find a new way. Albert Einstein once said, "*You cannot solve a problem with the same way of thinking that created it.*" You also cannot do the same thing, over and over again, and expect different results. Einstein described that as the definition of insanity. You need an entirely new approach and you need to stick with it. If you don't, your life will remain the same.

Most people do not change because they are failing to admit there is even a problem, but you are rising above this. I am excited for you because you are willing to take steps towards improving your life. You will succeed at whatever you put your mind to. I cannot wait to watch all of the wonderful things that are about to unfold in your life.

I have helped people who gave up on thinking they could be saved, and have accepted this as their way of life. I help people of all ages from all over the world. This is undoubtedly my life purpose. I have figured it out and want to share my journey with you. Since I began using these 7 steps, my life has catapulted forward. I am fully aware of my authentic self and live true to myself every day. It brings unlimited amounts of peace and joy to my life. I want to help you feel this same way.

My power within seems superhero-like. I feel strong enough to carry the weight of the world. I have used my strengths to lift others up through my blogging, magazine articles, quotes, seminar, life coaching, and throughout my daily life. I will help you through this. I want to minimize your regrets, guilt, and pain. You do not have to take as long as I did.

Wouldn't it be nice to free up more of your time for what matters most to you? You are never too young or too old to learn my steps and change your life around. I have recently helped a gentleman in his 80's find his inner strength for the first time in his life.

I have reached people who have completely isolated themselves for the majority of their lives. People who have deep trust issues, find themselves trusting me. I looked back for the reasons why I was able to touch these people's lives when no one else could, and there was a distinct pattern.

It was always the same process. If I had an idea of what their struggle was, I would open up first with one of my relevant experiences. I continued to go deep into my story so they could connect with me on an emotional level. I would then tell them my pivotal moment that changed the way I thought or acted. I would finish by telling them how it all ended up for me. This gave them hope. Sometimes, I would get a surprised look saying, *I never knew you had it that bad. I can surely tell you my story, as it seems like nothing in comparison to yours.*

I could write several books on many topics. In fact, I intend to. This is part of the reason why it took so long for my first book to come out. I had three books on the go and many more written in my head. I think that is what has always set me apart and provides me with my special gift. Whatever anyone is going through, I can relate on a deep level of sort. People feel like I have truly been there. I do not have a Ph.D., but I think without that piece of paper, I am more approachable and I am less intimidating. I can connect on the same level and really tune into the root of a problem. This allows me to make a greater impact on many lives.

NOTE TO SELF: EMPOWERMENT

For me to help you find your true self, purpose and power, I need to write my book the exact way I would as though you were right in front of me, searching for answers. I can only write it from a place of authenticity. Others may do it differently, but this is my unique way. These are my stories and experiences, which are different from anyone else's. I feel confident in my capabilities of helping you, the best way I know how.

I will be revealing aspects of myself that are relevant to each step. By sharing this, I am hoping that it will spare you from the many years of hardships I have endured. Each person learns differently and are at various stages along their path. By looking at my situations, things may resonate with you. It may create more awareness to your own situation and offer you some insight.

I will start disclosing my steps in Chapter 3, when I was at my rock bottom. That way, if you are there now, I am here to help lift you out. At the time, I did not realize that my life was heading downhill so quickly. I truly felt as though I was keeping it all together. I was always the strong one, who people turned to for strength. I stayed positive and optimistic. No matter what I went through, I could still manage to keep a smile on my face and a brave front. I became so good at it, that I even fooled myself.

I am going to help you achieve an extraordinary life. You will know more about who you are and what you want. When you know this, you will become more confident. With confidence, your inner strength will grow into an unstoppable force. You will be able to do and have whatever it is you desire in life.

If you are not at rock bottom, then give yourself a pat on the back because this will be much easier for you. You are already ahead of where I was, and your future looks much brighter than you think. We are going to move forward together, from whatever stage you are at.

If you feel you are good, hopefully you enjoy my stories. It is also beneficial to have these reminders to keep you from regressing. I believe everything happens for a reason, and that you are reading this book for a reason. Maybe you will need to turn to it in the future, or use it as a refresher to keep you on the right track? You may know someone who we can help out. Everyone needs inspiration and more positivity in their lives!

I figured I would start the process at my lowest point; when I was the furthest from my true self. When I felt powerless and I was stripped right down to the core of my being, yet still managed to find my way through. I had absolutely no clue how I was going to get myself out of this huge mess, yet I managed to fix myself from the inside out. This is the only way to create your solid foundation for an authentically happy and fulfilling life. I will guide you through the technique I used to change my entire life around. These are the same steps that deeply connected me to my unwavering truth, which fuels my unlimited power within. Let me help you access your true self and the personal power that leads to an extraordinary life.

The most important thing for you to know, is that **you are not alone.** Let's build you up from the inside first, so everything on the outside can fall into place. Let's make your foundation so strong and secure, that nothing can stop you. I am here for you throughout this entire journey and beyond. Please do not ever hesitate to reach out to me.

You need to invest time in yourself because you are worth it. Let's take action now. Your family and friends deserve to have you at your best, and you deserve it too.

2

WHO AM I?

My true self was not celebrated from the day of my birth. I was an unwanted and unplanned pregnancy. I know this because I was told several times. Even though I do not remember the day I was born, I believe my soul had been imprinted with this fact. I continued to carry the increasing weight of this burden. My mother was nineteen and my father was three years older. I was told by both my mother and father that they had only been dating for three months, before I started my human formation. The tragedy of this was not that I had prematurely forced two people to be together. The real disappointment was that I was born a girl.

This was made known my entire life by my father. I was the first born of what would later be a total of five girls for him, so you can imagine the pressures that I have felt. I began to crave nurturing and encouragement. I longed to be accepted and loved unconditionally. I wanted to be good enough for my father. I wanted to be worthy of his love.

Each day, a little piece of my soul and true self was corroded. Every day, I would lose another part of me and who I was meant to become. My father wanted a boy so I became a tomboy, the closest to a boy my father would ever get.

I was the fastest runner. When I was a young child, I could remember a woman behind me at the starting line of a race. I heard her commenting as she looked at my legs. "She has muscles like a man!" I remember thinking: *How could I have muscles like a man? I am not even a boy?* I excelled in whatever sport or activity I tried. I would prove to my father, that it did not matter that I was a girl. I could beat any boy. Anytime. Anywhere. Surely, he had to be proud of that? But, somehow I always fell short and I could always do better.

*****

It was the summer after completing first grade. School was out and it was time to have some fun. The sun was hot, yet inviting. I would notice the other second graders playing outside in their yards and enjoying their summer vacation. My father would have his stopwatch, while timing me racing around the block. I remember feeling embarrassed, as the other kids did not have to repeatedly run around the huge block in the beaming hot sun. Their soaking wet shirts were from cooling off in the sprinkler. Maybe I could pretend my sweaty shirt was from a sprinkler also?

It did not matter how hot or uncomfortable I was. "Just beat your last time." That was all that was important to my father. Several times I would run around the block in hopes of shaving off my time. My friends would want to play with me, but I could not afford to stop. I also wanted to play, but each second counted.

I hated running. Still to this day, I hate running. I had no choice. If my father ordered me to run; I ran. I would not stop, unless he told me to stop. It did not matter how hot, uncomfortable, or dehydrated I was. I could not decide which I liked better...running throughout my summer vacation or going to school?

My father was a teacher, so I was constantly being monitored. If I did not hand something in, he knew it. I never felt smart enough compared to my father, who seemed to know everything. When quizzed above grade level questions, I failed to know the answers. He would proudly give the correct answer. I never understood how this was such a fun game, as it always resulted in me feeling stupid.

I was a tall, skinny, scrawny kid, with muscles in my legs like a man. It did not seem fair that my sister was not forced to do the same boyish things and build awkward, masculine muscles. I think that idea was scrapped when it was clear that she could never surpass my abilities. I had almost two extra years of intense training and conditioning, so it would be near impossible for her to catch up. You would be an idiot not to focus and place your bet on this racehorse!

There was always a sense of jealousy and resentment when my sister looked at me. I could only assume that she never felt good enough also. She never got as much grief from my father when she wanted to do girly things. We both wanted to take dance lessons like all the other girls our age. All I heard was, "Why would you want to take dancing? The only way that will help you is if you are going to grow up and be a stripper. Do you want to grow up and be a STRIPPER!?" Clearly at 9 years old I was not thinking about my career path, but I am quite positive that being a stripper was not one of my top choices. I can guarantee you, it was not my motive for wanting to join dance. Could I not do what I wanted for once? I thought being a child was supposed to be fun and carefree? My childhood seemed so rigid and structured in comparison. There was no room for my opinion and input.

I grew up believing that my sister, Stacy was prettier than me. She had long, blonde hair and blue eyes like my mother. I desperately wanted to inherit the same blue eyes like everyone else in my family. Instead, I was the only one who got my father's *green* eyes and I resented that fact. I wanted to be like my mother. My biggest nightmare would have been to grow up and resemble my dad. He was surely not the role model I admired. I was mortified when people I knew would see him coach basketball. Guaranteed, you would see my father on the sidelines screaming at the players at the top of his lungs. His face would be pitch red. The pressure of his boiling blood would extend from his face, all the way to the top of his bald head.

Even though I was paper thin, my father would repeatedly tell me that I was fat. It never made any sense to me because my friends were calling me skinny. When I looked in the mirror, I could not see the fat he was talking about. I finally stood up to my dad and said, "I am not fat." When I hit him with this reality, he replied back, "Well wait until you have two kids, then you will be fat." His words haunted me for several years. I did not want to be fat after having two children.

As a child, I felt ugly, unwanted, unloved, and worthless. Even trying to achieve perfection was still not adequate. I became withdrawn and extremely shy. I would be the child who would put her head down when spoken to. I could feel the blushing heat in my cheeks from the embarrassment. It would almost get as red as my father's face during a rage.

I did not show signs of being afraid of him though, because my innate sense of inner strength was stronger than my fear. I took on the role of protector. I was always there to defend my two sisters, against his quick temper. It didn't matter that he towered over me. My spirit was strong and wanted desperately to be free. My inner strength has always been my source to help me through many obstacles in my life. Nothing could break me down. The things he would say to me did hurt, but I would never let him know that. I felt like I was always doing something wrong and I would get spanked for it. I understand that other parents spanked their children back then, but it seemed like it was happening way more often to me. My sessions seemed much longer and more aggressive. I actually remember the exact moment when I was blessed with this gift and tool that I would need to turn to several times throughout my life.

Something magical happened…I felt no pain. It could have been because I was in so much agony that I became numb, but it seemed more than that. I truly believe that the grace of God granted me with a gift. He was clearly aware of my grander plan, and could foresee that I would desperately need to use this gift as a protective measure, many times throughout my life. God does not give you more than you can handle, so at a very young age I learned to block out pain. I clearly could not survive without this ability. *From that moment on, I could instantly switch to survival mode and block the hurtful things out. I became immune to physical and mental pain.*

*****

Fourteen years old is a crucial age for adolescents. They are trying to figure out who they are and where they fit in. I was no different, except that I faced a few extra challenges. It was the summer before entering high school and my parents had been separated for a few years now. My mother's poor choices in men had finally caught up to her. She got herself into a dilemma. She kept trying to break it off with her boyfriend Dave, but his violent and controlling nature would not allow this.

I remember going home late one night from my best friend Robin's house. As I was entering my driveway, I could hear the loud sound of air coming out from the tires of my mom's car. It was dark, but I could see Dave slashing her tires. He was caught in the act and had some lame excuse.

Nights later, I was supposed to be sleeping, but I was listening to the Toronto Blue Jays baseball game on the radio. I could hear yelling outside my bedroom, which I thought was my mother cheering for the game. But then I heard it during a lull in the game, which did not warrant yelling or cheering. I soon realized that it was my mom's furious boyfriend. He was screaming at my mother and was clearly physically hurting her. The helplessness I felt, reminded me of when I was a young child. I wanted to speak out and protect my mother, but I never felt strong enough. Plus, she was the adult. I mistakenly thought she could protect herself and make her own healthy choices.

I was supposed to be sleeping, so I could not show signs of being awake. My mother would have been mortified and completely humiliated if she knew that I heard what was going on. She spent her life trying to protect us three girls by constantly sheltering us. She wanted to try and keep us oblivious to the cruel world outside. Her world could be crashing down and we would never know it.

The next day, as my mother was driving me to dance lessons, I never said a word. I knew what was going on though. I knew that she was trying desperately to escape this violent, abusive man. I also knew that she was falling for another man, who was a friend of his. He turned out to be an even worse choice, but that is a whole other story.

Dave was aware of this plan to leave him and was wondering if it was for the love of another. After our three or four hour drive from Sudbury, we returned to our home in Timmins. Our front door was left wide open in the middle of the freezing cold, Northern Ontario winter. I noticed the concerned look in my mother's eyes and knew it wasn't good. It was as if she knew who had done this. Was our house burglarized? My mother, two sisters and I cautiously walked into our home to find out.

Everything seemed to be in place and in the same way that we had left it, until we entered my mother's bedroom. Every single one my mother's photographs that she had ever owned were gone. All of our childhood pictures and family pictures. Any pictures of special occasions or holidays. Anything that held sentimental value to my mother. The only other items missing were all of my mom's diaries. All of her personal and intimate thoughts were violated and taken from her. This was clearly Dave's doing. He wanted to stick it right to my mother's heart, where it hurt most. If she was determined to leave him, then he wanted to internally destroy her.

My mother decided that we needed to get up and leave this town. Not only that, I could not tell anyone where I was moving to. Even if I wanted to, I couldn't because I had no clue what the plan was. I don't even think my mother knew what she was going to do. Although she had an extremely successful catering business, our safety was more important.

At the time my father still lived in Timmins. He was going to move to Mexico, and my mom, sisters and I were going to move to who knows where. I became extremely fond of the Poirier family who I babysat for, and I did not want to abandon them. I also did not want to leave my friends. I was shy and withdrawn, but I still had some close friends. And friends are your whole life at that age! High school is hard enough as it is, and now I was going to have to go to a school where I knew absolutely no one.

We were to go on one last trip with my father before his big move. We all packed for a three week road trip to Mexico. This gave my mother a few weeks to come up with a quick scheme and move all our stuff to our new, undisclosed location. She made plans to have a couple run her thriving catering business. That way, Dave could not find and murder all of us - as he had threatened my mother.

On our plane ride back to the Toronto Airport, I remember the passenger next to me asking the natural question, "Where do you live?" It was awkward not being able to answer such a simple question. "I don't know, but I will find out soon I hope."

From the airport, we drove to this house that literally looked like a castle. It had a turret with a spiral staircase. It had an indoor *and* outdoor pool, five bedrooms, five bathrooms, a three car garage, a sauna, and the list goes on. We were secluded in the country, owning 37 ½ acres of land. This was our new house? I guess I could handle living here…

There was a catch. My name would no longer be Trina Hall. I would have to legally change my name to my mother's new boyfriend's last name, whom I had only met once before. His last name obviously meant nothing to me, because he meant nothing to me. It seemed odd that we had to go and make sworn statements that he adopted us, in order to legally change all of our last names. We are adopted now? We have different names? Did my sisters and I even have a say in this? Once again, I felt powerless. It was already done before we had any time to question it. We were now living in the country somewhere in Southern Ontario, over seven hours away from where we once called home. All this to ensure that Dave could not locate us via the Provincial School Records, which he had access to.

If I was not allowed to be my true self before, I was starting to really get unsure about my identity now. The first day of high school was particularly difficult. I remember I must have gotten confused and wrote my old last name on one sheet, and my new last name on another. My teacher asked me, "Who are you?"

To tell you the truth, I had no clue who I was at that moment. I was trying to figure things out like every other adolescent. Also, my entire life as I knew it was stripped from under me in an instant. I was not allowed to contact my old friends. I had disappeared and vanished out of all their lives without a trace.

At lunch, the students would group together with people they already knew from their previous elementary schools. That way they did not look uncool and alone, the way I looked. I knew nobody.

I was not happy that I couldn't contact my old friends. I couldn't say, do or feel whatever I wanted. I showed no emotions. I have been so used to masking them, that it became second nature. I wasn't even sure that I had feelings anymore. I became numb and even more distant. Not only on command either, this now became part of my character. I didn't have too many friends during the first couple of years of high school. I had 15 years of secrets and emotions bottled up inside of me. One day, during the middle of class, these intense emotions burst out of me.

I was halfway through 10th grade, and without any warning, I was about to cry. This was foreign to me, as I was never allowed to cry. I can honestly say that I do not remember crying even once before in my life. Not as a child and most certainly not as a teenager. So what triggered my outburst of tears on this particular day, still remains a mystery to me.

I bolted out of the classroom to spare humiliation. My teacher must have been concerned for my well-being, because he sent a student from my class to follow me into the bathroom. This person was a stranger to me, as the majority of all the students still were. I was sitting on the bathroom floor, as this kind classmate knelt down to console me. I let it all out. I mean ALL of it. All the things I promised my mother that I could never share. All these feelings and thoughts that I was never allowed to freely express. I did not spare one single detail during my rant. It felt incredibly good to release everything that I wasn't even embarrassed. She was overwhelmed with all the shocking details that her only response was, "You should write a book." I will always remember this because it validated the strong feeling I had when I was 10 years old, that I would someday write a book. I also found it odd that at age fifteen, this stranger felt I had enough content from my short lifetime to fill an entire book. I do not know who this angel of a classmate was who listened to me that day, but I want to say, *"Thank you. You made me feel so much better. I needed to release all those secrets that I have been holding inside of me."*

Besides all the secrets, hiding, and running from drama, I did not like my new last name. So much that I am not going to even mention it in this book. It turned out I was never even legally adopted. My new last name wasn't ever my last name. I looked like a fool when I was trying to get my driver's license. I was applying in my new name, but they would not issue it until I showed them my adoption certificate. Until I provided proof, they would have to go back to my old name, Trina Hall, since that is the name stated on my birth certificate. My mother never provided me with a certificate and it did not take me long to figure out that we were not adopted. There I was again, stuck between two names. It was difficult to remember which name to use where. I told my sister and we became distraught by this discovery. "Are we even sisters?" We started questioning everything. We felt like our entire lives were a lie. We felt like puppets, playing this role in this new life that my mother created.

We all come to a point in our lives when we ask, "Who am I?" This is a common question when we are trying to figure out our true selves and true purpose in life. It is exceptionally young to ask this question at seventeen. This was the first time that I was ever really hit hard with this.

I realized then, that I did not know who I was. I was living a life trying to please everyone else. I was trying hard to meet each and every expectation of me. I felt as though I was not allowed to think for myself, as my thoughts did not seem to matter. The only way I could safely express them was when I was alone in my room. My paper and pen were my only confidant. Each soothing stroke of my pen would make the pain a little more bearable. I could always count on my writing to comfort me. I wanted to avoid confrontation and I did not want to upset anyone, so this was my only outlet. I did not like drama, as my life already had enough of it.

The drama never stopped. I endured one struggle after another. I was always busy and never had time to deal with much. I became a mother at 21 years old. As a mother, your needs are secondary and your child takes precedence. I had no problem with this transition as my needs, thoughts, beliefs, and passions were already used to taking a back seat.

My mother was ecstatic when she became a grandmother. She was always there for Jasmine, Brooklyn and I. I looked up to my mom. All my friends would comment on how beautiful she was. Her amazing inner strength was a characteristic that was passed on to me. My mother always acted like nothing was ever wrong, but it was impossible to try and blind us from our tumultuous world. She would say one thing, but we would see something conflicting. I started to have a distorted sense of the world around me because we were constantly sheltered in a bubble. It was difficult to figure out what was true, from what was not. There was too much denial and everything was locked in an emotional vault. My mother died keeping silent about most of her 48 years of secrets and struggles.

*****

The physical and mental abuse I encountered in my life, helped me further master how to block out pain. There was nothing anyone could say or do anymore to hurt me. Actually...I need to bite my tongue. The sexual assault, at age 33, was a tough blow and was the only exemption from my mastery.

Naturally the Friday morning afterwards, I was unable to work. I still pushed myself to go, but the excruciating pain made it difficult for me to sit down at my desk. Within 20 minutes at work, my mind focused back to replaying the night before. The fogginess lifted and things became crystal clear. I had been drugged and raped.

I had spent about twelve hours in the hospital. When I returned home, I stayed in bed and cried for most of the weekend. On Saturday, I was unable to attend my eldest daughter, Jasmine's dance competition. I was dying inside because I had never missed anything my daughters had. I gathered my strength on Sunday to attend Brooklyn's First Communion. She is my baby and would never understand me missing her important day. A person close to the family expressed concern for me to my sister. "What happened to Trina? She looks as white as a ghost!" I must have looked horrible, but I was not in any state to care at that time. I pretended like nothing was wrong. It was quite easy for me to do, as I have watched my mother do this her entire life.

My boss was surprised to see me at work on Monday. She offered me a free two week counselling program and time off work. I never took time for myself, so why would I start now? I was a single mother of two. I could not afford to slow down, let alone...break down.

3

STEP 1: DISCOVER YOUR TRUTH

There I was, alone in my room at rock bottom. The lowest point possible in life. Any lower and I would be 6-feet under. Trust me, I briefly thought about it. I was a failure and a disappointment. It started when I was born, and here I was back again. Did my life go full circle? Was this the end for me? At this point I was worth more dead than alive. I was physically and emotionally fading away to nothing. I was extremely stressed and malnourished. The cheap pasta that would have been used to hide my protruding ribs was being used to feed my two girls. Pretty soon I would no longer be able to afford that either. I felt like I had nothing more to offer them...or anybody.

My downward spiral began when my sister Stacy was in a rush to sell her business and needed to get rid of it within three weeks. She told me there was another potential buyer, so I felt extra pressured and rushed to make a decision. I believed that the sales were amazing and that it would be a low risk investment. I reminded my sister of our past and made it strongly known that I could not afford to be screwed over. It was not just me involved. This decision would also affect her two nieces, as I was taking pretty much all of the equity out of my house to give to her.

The business was doomed from the start and inevitably failed. My lawyer seemed against me purchasing this business and even tried to stall me, just before my best friend and I signed the papers. He asked, "Are you sure you want to do this?" My final words were, "Yes. I trust my sister." In hindsight, I should have known better, considering there was a 20 year history telling me otherwise.

Around 18 months later, in 2009, I was stripped of my life and my identity. I had no money and no job. I was losing my possessions one by one. Because there was a crash in the housing market and I took the money out of my house to purchase the business, Jasmine, Brooklyn and I were only weeks away from the foreclosing of our house.

I have already lost my mother to cancer. She was one of the few people who I felt truly loved me. Now I was losing the only part of her that I was desperately trying to hold on to. I had used the inheritance money I had received from my mother to buy this house. I always felt like each wall that surrounded me was a representation of my mother's warm embrace. My mother always wanted the best for me and her money allowed me to buy the only house I have ever owned. It was in a nice neighborhood. We felt safe and protected.

NOTE TO SELF: EMPOWERMENT

My life was like a scene from the movie, *Titanic*. With the sad violins playing in the background, as our ship was sinking. I felt like the mother who was calmly reading her children a bedtime story. Trying to relax and soothe them, to keep them oblivious of what was really going on. I had to stay strong, but I had reached a point when I was forced to face my reality. I could no longer pretend like everything was okay. I was running out of hope and it was getting harder to stay positive. I did not know who I could trust. I could not even trust myself with my own judgement and choices. I started to get really scared. I have been through various struggles many times before, and I could always depend on myself to get out of them. This was the first time things were different. I truly did not think I could do it again. I came *too* close, *too* many times. Maybe this time I could no longer be saved? There was little strength left in me and I became worried.

My world was being completely destroyed as I knew it. My excellent credit score was being demolished. I was losing most of my material possessions, my pride, my business, my money and my house. I had been there for many people during my lifetime and I would rarely ask for anything myself. Once I became financially bankrupt and had nothing left to give, most of my friends were gone also.

I was so used to having people lie to me, I did not know what was true anymore. I was so used to pretending everything would be fine, that I did not allow myself to admit that it was not. I was so used to pleasing others and avoiding confrontation, that I never had the chance to figure out what I truly wanted. I would try and give these people the benefit of the doubt, but things were not adding up. I longed for people to be *real*. I was craving authenticity. I welcomed the mistakes, flaws, quirks, bad habits…I welcomed it all. *I begged for the truth.* No matter how much it hurt, I wanted the truth. At least I could make better informed decisions. Most of my prior decisions were based on lies and that clearly was not working for me. I am sure that I would not have made the same mistakes if the truth was fully disclosed to me. At least, I would hope not. If people showed me their true colors right up front, things would have been different. If I was not told continuous lies and cover-ups, I would have known what I was dealing with. I would have not played the role of the fool so many times. I would not be spending most of my time shaking my head, while calling myself stupid. Between all of the hard hits on the head and the constant head shaking, it is no wonder I suffered from what I call a *spiritual concussion*.

MY SPIRITUAL CONCUSSION/COMA

This has been caused by being hit over the head way too many times with too many hard lessons. I have been repeatedly knocked down, until I was eventually knocked out. I woke up to my life completely destroyed as I knew it. How did I get here? I am hoping that I reach you before you get to rock bottom, so I can spare you from the added grief. But if you are already there, I will help you. There is still hope, so do not give up now! You made it this far, and it only gets better from here on out.

NOTE TO SELF: EMPOWERMENT

Life gives you whispers. If you do not listen to them, then they become louder and hit harder. The Universe does not mess around. You are put on this earth to learn lessons, so have faith in knowing this: *There are no mistakes. There are only lessons to be learned in divine order, preparing you for your life's purpose.*

The Bible states, "The truth shall set you free." I was prepared to face it. I figured it would be worth the short-term pain to avoid a lifetime of misery. When the truth started revealing itself to me, I almost immediately regretted my wish. I did not realize how much it would hurt. All the betrayal, the lies, and bad decisions I had made came forward. I spent the next few months shaking my head in disbelief. I do not know how many times I said, "I am so stupid." I cannot believe that I trusted all these unworthy people. I could not believe that I put up with all the things I did. I had so many questions. It was like I woke up from a coma and was trying to orientate myself. What was allowing me to stay in these situations? How did my life get so far off track?

One by one, my truths were revealed to me. The gift I was given to not feel any pain was no longer working for me, and I could no longer protect myself. *I felt all the years of pain that I had escaped my entire life.* It took a long time to recover from my spiritual concussion. My world came crashing down and it was too much to bear. It took every ounce of inner strength, but my strength was gone also. It had been pulled out from underneath me. All the decades of corrosion had finally worn me down. For the first time in my life, I felt there was no way out. No matter what I went through in the past, I could always count on my inner strength to pull me through it. This time, I wasn't sure if I could do it *again*.

When I could no longer count on myself, I knew I was in trouble. I was my biggest ally, and now look where I am at. I could not trust my choices and my judgement. If I was not strong enough to pull myself out of this one, who would? I was alone and I trusted no one. I could not repair all this damage fast enough. There was not even a piece of me left to hold on to.

You cannot afford to tempt fate and lose strength. You need to practice great self-care. This is where I went wrong. Because I have triumphed over many obstacles, I felt like I could overcome anything. You can only do this if you are at your full capacity. Once you allow people to chip away at you, they can find a weak spot and take you down. Do not take a chance on allowing others to take away your power.

During this 18 month financial demise, I started to become depressed and scared. I was suffering from chronic stress. A lifetime of hard hits on the head, with all of my lessons learned, eventually took its toll. Something had to change, but I had no clue what to do. The continuous shaking my head in disbelief did not help the healing. As the truth unveiled, I became increasingly aware of my foolish choices.

I felt like I was asleep my entire life. How did I allow myself to get here? My life would never be the same. Now that I have woken up, I can never go backwards and I can never "sleep" again. Even if I wanted to, I couldn't. I needed to recover, while in unbearable internal suffering. All of the hurt and pain was no longer numbed by my spiritual coma. I never imagined that everything I was unable to face, would all resurface simultaneously.

In a matter of minutes, a bunch of truths, revelations and thoughts flooded my head. These are the ones I remember:

My Truth #1

I had become my mother. I was making the same mistakes and continued all the same vicious cycles with bad choices in men. (Sorry to all the nice guys I turned down. I was not ready for you then). I was so busy idolizing my mother that I became unaware of the harmful patterns and beliefs that were being transferred to me. *Realizing this truth helped me to break this cycle with my own children.*

My mother often warned me to always keep a close eye on my drink, but I let my guard down the older I got. She would tell me her story about what happened to her as an adult, after her drink had been spiked. I did not think it would happen to me at 33 years old. You would never think something that horrible would happen in the presence of your own boyfriend, but I had to face the truth. I had been drugged and gang-raped.

About a year or two later, I was watching the Hillary Swank movie, *Boys Don't Cry*, with my close friend Mark. During a certain scene, I broke down. I could not handle the visual reminder of what had happened to me. It was then, I decided I needed to get some counselling.

My Truth #2

I used to be surrounded by people when things were good and I had more to give them. Now where were they all? Almost all the phone calls I was receiving were from bill collectors. That was a huge wake-up call. You really find out who your friends are and who really cares for you during times like this.

My Truth #3

I let my best friend down. Although it was unintentional, the truth is I did. She trusted me when going half in with purchasing the business, and I trusted my sister. As a result, this also affected her life. I had guilt and regrets that weighed heavily on me.

My Truth #4

I could no longer pretend like everything was okay because they were definitely not. I am going to have to learn to open up and ask for help. I would have to swallow my pride.

My Truth #5

My poor choices were not only affecting me, but also my children and everyone around me. I caused people pain. I did not trust myself to make a healthy choice.

My Truth #6

I am not crazy like people were trying to make me believe. They would much rather put the blame onto me, instead of taking responsibility for their own wrongdoings. *The truth makes sense, and all the lies I was being told did not.* I am kind-hearted, honest, and loving. It is okay that I am a girl. I am worthy of being loved. I am good enough, just the way I am.

My Truth #7

To me, my father is not like my friends' father. I heard of fathers loving their daughters and doing anything for them. I heard sayings throughout my life like, "She daddy's little girl". I never experienced this firsthand, but I thought, what the heck?

    I e-mailed my father in a desperate plea for help. Truthfully, I was not expecting anything, but I wanted to give him a chance to step up as a father, instead of assuming the worst of him. I asked to borrow $10,000 so his two grandchildren and I would be able to keep our house. In his response, he stated that he was "choosing" not to help me. He thought the best thing was for me to "learn how to fish, instead of giving me a fish". Obviously he didn't know his first-born daughter very well, as I have been *fishing* for myself my entire life. I had been *fishing* so hard that I just needed someone to throw me a fish to give me enough energy to go back out there *fishing* again. I understand that my sister, who had until recently been mostly absent from his life, has now made an effort to contact him. He knew I was losing everything and we would have no place to live, yet he chose not to help us.

My Truth #8

My life was full of my mistakes. The only two things I felt I did right was help a lot of people and be an amazing mother.

My Truth #9

My life was not good. I had only a few weeks to find a place to live. I could not trust or count on most of the people in my life. I barely had any friends or family to turn to, and my options were very slim to none. I had to consider the fact that my daughters and I may have to live on the street.

My Truth #10

Times were getting pretty desperate. I had a few choices that would go against my moral fiber. There was a man who was fond of me and very well-off that owned a few houses and cars. My sister Stacy advised me to go for him as a solution to my situation. Of course when you are desperate and are weeks away from being homeless, the thought would naturally cross your mind. He had a house and it was better than living on the street, right? We could live with him as a friend? Well, I couldn't do it. I decided to stay true to myself and if that meant we had to live on the street, I guess I would have to accept that fate.

I was also tempted with cheating people out of some money and they would never have known. My girls and I desperately needed money for food and basic living, but I

NOTE TO SELF: EMPOWERMENT

still couldn't do it. My morals have always been something that I would never compromise. *(Looking back, this is one of my proudest decisions. I was tested and had people angry with me, yet I stayed true to who I was. I did not compromise myself or my morals in the slightest).*

*****

These were some of my truths that I had to deal with. I was forced to think about all the things that I did not have the time to think about. I was too busy rushing through life and working a full-time job. I would rush home to feed my two girls and bring them to all their lessons. Often times, I did not even have time to stop. I would leave work, quickly pick up a $5.00 already cooked pizza, and call my girls to warn them that I was coming for the "drive-by". They would be waiting for me at the end of our driveway and my car would barely come to a rolling stop, as my girls jumped in.

    Once their activities were over, I would help them with homework. I truly do not know how I did it all. It did not bother me, since it kept me occupied. I didn't have to deal with my unhealed issues and I would not have to face all the things that were hurting me deep down inside. I honestly did not even know that I was hurting. I got so good at masking my feelings, I fooled myself for all of these years.

I was thankful to have the truth slap me in the face. I asked for the truth and boy did it hurt. I became aware of what was around me. I guess I was being protected before because I was not ready to face and accept the truth as it really was. That is why many of us are in denial. I just thought that I was being a positive person and looking for the good in people. I would justify people's bad behavior and would make excuses for them. Eventually, I had to accept it for what it was. I became aware of more truths as time went on. When the truth is revealed, you can make healthier, better choices. Even though it hurt, this was the best thing for me. I was well on my way to becoming free…and becoming "me"!

THE SHIFT

Instead of continuing to be the victim, I turned everything around on me and shifted the blame. I started to take responsibly for my past actions and choices. It did not feel very good, but slowly I began to feel like I had a sense of control over my life. My life did not rely on what others did or said to me. I had a choice. Why did I stay? Why didn't I say anything? Why did I believe them? *I stopped listening to what I was being told, and I started listening to me.*

DISCOVER YOUR TRUTH

Discovering your truth is the first step, and the first step is always the hardest. This is the one I am going to spend the most time with you on, because it is the most crucial. I am warning you now, some stuff may be hard to swallow –

especially if you discover that you have been betrayed by a partner, family member, co-worker, or friend. I am not trying to scare you, I am trying to help you. I need to tell you this in order to prepare you, so you know exactly what you will be dealing with. When you know this beforehand, it will be easier to work through it. You may feel like a fool for falling for lies. It is not going to be fun when you find out that people are not who they said they were. You may become disappointed or devastated as people's true colors are revealed in front of you.

When you are in a bad situation, it is difficult to look beyond the moment and see the big picture. I will help bring you clarity. If you can gather whatever strength you have and make it over this hump, things will start to turn around for the better. You will never have to go back there again and redo this step. The healing and self-awareness which you will receive through this, will be *life transforming.* You will be happy once you made it through.

How do you figure out the truth if you are constantly being told lies? Some people lie to cover up wrongdoings or bad habits. They may feel they are protecting you from getting hurt, when in the end, it hurts you even more. Some people are so convincing, that you may start questioning yourself. Do not allow people to make you feel like you are wrong or crazy, when you know the truth. You can feel it when people are not being real. *The truth makes sense. Lies and fake people do not.*

Many people are afraid of being authentic and showing their true selves. They create false fronts, in order to be accepted and impress others. Maybe you are afraid of revealing your true self in fear of being judged? Very often, we are afraid to admit the truth of how bad a situation is to ourselves. We may remember how good it *used* to be, but maybe we need to face the fact that things have changed? In the end the truth always comes out, so we may as well get it over with and deal with it now.

    I do not want you to hit rock bottom like me, in order for you to face your truth. Even if you think your life is perfect. In fact, especially if you think your life is perfect, it is important for you to do these exercises. You need to take time to deal with this. You may surprise yourself and feel things you never knew you felt, or think things you never knew you thought. You may have thought you moved on from something, and discover that there is another layer.

    I am sharing these steps to make it easier for you, because life is hard enough as it is. If you are like me, you learn everything the hard way. Why make things more difficult than they have to be? I am giving you the tools to move past this. Remember, I am here with you every step of the way. I know it requires taking some time out of your busy schedule, but it is imperative that you do. You cannot afford not to. You will save several years or possibly a lifetime of hardships if you deal with this now. It is time to get out of the habit of ignoring your own wants and needs. It is not working for you any longer, so let's explore this together. If you want things to change and get better, there is no avoiding this step.

    The reason I say to discover *your* truth is because you have people around you telling you different things and conflicting stories, making it hard to even think straight. You may also be surrounded by negative people, who are criticizing you and constantly putting you down. You may start to have a distorted sense of self. You need to remove yourself from this chaos so you can start to think clearly. It is crucial that you quiet your world down. We need to get to the bottom of this and right down to the root of the problem. We need to figure this out. Otherwise we are only dealing with the symptoms.

Forget about what is right or wrong. Really dig deep and find your truth. How do you truly feel? What do you really think? This is *your* truth and *your* perspective. Do not let anyone sway you from that. Once we figure that out, then we can move forward and improve your life dramatically. You will be well equipped to make healthier decisions.

If you faced the fact that someone was lying to you, you would most likely make different decisions. Do not be afraid to expose all the truths. You want this. As much as it may hurt or disappoint you, embrace this process.

For example, say you thought your partner was cheating on you. Regardless of whether that was true or not, it is true to you. This is a part of your reality. Because you think he is cheating, you do not trust him. Anxiety hits when this person shows up late from work. You interrogate and become uneasy. Ultimately, your relationship will be doomed because there is no trust. This person could be the most loyal person in the world, but it doesn't matter. What matters is what you think because this is your reality. This is what we need to deal with and improve upon, so you can see things as they truly are. We do not want to wreck something good because we are transferring over our past hurts and worries. But if they really are cheating, do not let them make you believe that you are paranoid because of your past either.

The same is true, if the tables were turned. You may be in a relationship where you feel you are constantly trying to prove yourself. They may have issues with trust and you are constantly trying to prove your love or your worthiness. Until they work out their issues, you will always fall short. You will never be good enough or worthy enough. This is the truth and it is a cruel wake-up call.

You are strong enough to deal with your truths. You are tired of the way things are. You may feel like nothing is ever going to change because it has been this way for so long. They *are* going to change and your life will be better than you could ever imagine. I believe in you and I want the best for you. Let's create the life you desire.

EMBRACE AND ACCEPT THE TRUTH

It is always best to have the facts. When you see people or situations for what they really are, you can make a more informed decision. It will be based on truth, instead of lies. If you are struggling to figure out what is true, always go with what you feel deep down inside.

AVOID DENIAL

Avoiding the truth prolongs the inevitable. The truth will continue to nag at you until you decide to face it. Have the courage to deal with it head on. The sooner the better.

You do not want to look back, shaking your head at all the time you have wasted.

STAND IN YOUR TRUTH

Be true to who you are. Do not be afraid to stand up for what you believe in, or what you feel is right. You will attract the people who will unconditionally love you, just as you are.

SCHEDULE IN SOME "ME" TIME

Do yourself a favor and make sure you schedule time for yourself.

- Be alone in a quiet room. You should give yourself some time to think clearly and re-evaluate your life.
- Meditate. This releases stress and gives you a chance to breathe.
- Find someone to babysit your kids. Go to a quiet park. Go do yoga. Get a massage. It does not matter what it is, you need to take some time for just you.
- Go for a walk in nature or by water. This will help bring you back to yourself.

Take the time to be by yourself. It is important that you have no external distractions telling you how you should think, feel, or act. How do you *really* feel? Be truthful and honest with yourself. There is no need for masks or pretending...be real. It can be a hard reality, but you will have the truth in front of you. This will help you become clear on what is no longer serving you.

It is imperative that you spend quiet time alone and self-reflect. It is important to reach a deep understanding of what is causing you to make unhealthy choices, so you will not repeat them.

FEEL THE PAIN

Allow yourself to feel your emotions and work yourself through them. It will get so much better once you come out the other side.

ACCEPT YOUR REALITY

People come and go in your life. Circumstances do not always stay the same. Your whole life could be turned upside down, which could cause you to lose your entire identity. You might not like it or agree with it, but it may be your reality. You can either continue to ignore this, or we can figure out a solution as to where to go from here.

WRITE DOWN YOUR TRUTHS

So, what is *your* truth? Write it down. Not what others are telling you is true. Not what you were conditioned to believe. Do not think of how you *should* feel or how other people *expect* you to feel. It is irrelevant what others have told you was the truth. What matters is what you believe and how you perceive things. Your truth is affecting your life and your choices, which shapes your reality.

No one is around. You are by yourself. Allow your emotions and thoughts to flow. The truth makes sense, so what makes sense to you? Do not worry about what is right or wrong. Write down how you feel with no judgements. Let's get straight to your facts. You do not even need to understand why you are feeling certain things during this time. Process them as they come.

    If you truly do not love someone, allow yourself to feel that. If someone is hurting you, then acknowledge it. If you do not trust someone, it is as simple as that. You may discover that certain people have used you, manipulated you, and have lied to you. You may have to come to terms with the fact that people who you have always been there for, are not there for you when you finally need them. You may realize some of your own past actions that you are not pleased with. Try not to get caught up in all the emotions of this. Try to detached yourself and keep as objective as you can. It is our emotions and fears that prevent us from dealing with the truth. We may be giving out great advice, which we should be taking ourselves. We can do this because we feel like we are not dealing with our problems directly. This is similar to writing our problems in third person. Use this method for the hurtful moments or stuff we kept hidden for a long period of time. When we find out what we don't like and want, then we know that the opposite is what we do like and want.

NOTE TO SELF: EXERCISES

Picture yourself looking at your life from above and write what you see. Write your story in third person as though it is happening to someone else other than you. This will help you get an objective view of the truth, with the least amount of emotions getting in the way of this process.

Next:

- Take out a piece of paper or your journal.
- Draw a line done the middle of the page.
- On the right side, write the heading "What I don't like/want".
- On the left side, write "What I do like/want".

Once you have this list, we can start to think of solutions to these things, so you can ultimately be happy in all areas of your life.

- Write down all of the things in your life that you are not happy with and that you want to change.
- Write down your list of truths. I gave you plenty of examples of mine. What are yours? Do not hold back. Remember, it is only you that will see what you wrote. You need to work things through, so we can start to get really clear of who you truly are and want you truly want.

HEAL YOUR INNER CHILD

Our personality is formed by the age of seven. Children naturally model after their parents. Traditions, expectations, and beliefs get passed down throughout the generations, without much thought or questioning. It simply is the way it has always been. How you were raised and your type of childhood, often carries into your adulthood. Your self-esteem and self-worth is either nurtured or damaged during these early years. This causes us to grow up thinking that we are not good enough. We may grow up becoming *perfectionists* and we will still be hard on ourselves. We will also become *people pleasers*, in order to gain acceptance and the love we craved as a child. Because we are trying to just get by in the moment, we do not even think about or dig up what has happened to us all those years ago.

Pull out your journal again. The act of writing is cathartic. Express all of your earliest memories of when you were a child on paper. Focus on the ones with both of your parents, or lack of.

- How did they make you feel?
- Did they make you feel loved?
- Did they make you feel secure?
- What were your fondest memories?
- What were your worst memories?
- Were they there for you?
- How did your parents treat each other?
- If your parents are not together, how were their relationships?
- How do you feel you are most like your mother?
- How do you feel you are most like your father?
- Is there anything you feel is not healed from your childhood?

After these questions are answered, you may notice some patterns or cycles. You may be living your mother's or father's life by default. Is this how you really want to be? Is there something you want to change? Awareness of this is what will allow you to make different choices.

If you came to discover that the reason you are not feeling like you are good enough stems from one of your parents, we can turn this around also. You are good enough, just as you are. From this day forward, we are going to make a conscious effort to remove all negative self-talk. We will replace these negative words and memories, with positive thoughts or affirmations. They do not have any power over you, now that you are taking your power back. We are going to build yourself up to the point where you love yourself. When you are comfortable in your own skin and find self-love, others will love you back. You get out what you put in.

It will take a lot of inner work on your part, but it will be well worth it in the end. After completing this step, you will have discovered the real you. This is your true self. You have been hiding from this person for so long, that you may not even know he/she existed. This is your authentic self, who you need to embrace. Own it. People may have a hard time adjusting to this "new" you, but this is the person God designed to put out in this world. You are different than everyone else and have your own unique gifts and characteristics to offer the world. You are perfect, just as you are. You can work on growing and self-improvement, but this is only to enhance and become the best version of you. You got this!

4

STEP 2: TRUST YOURSELF

I was stripped down to my bare bones - both metaphorically and physically. I had been corroded down to only the core of my being, with no more masks...just me. I was vulnerable and humble. I had completely lost my dignity and pride. My ego was shattered along with it. My world as I have always known it, was gone. It was like a tornado had swept through my entire life and demolished everything. I was left with nothing but my authentic self and my truth.

    I looked at this as a gift, as it forced me to see everything as it really was. I was fully exposed and I no longer had the will to pretend, make excuses, or hide. There was only the truth right in front of me. I had no choice, but to accept things as they were. The truth was clear and there was no denying it. Each time I tried, I would get slapped in the face with it again. Even though I did not want to believe it, I had to trust myself.

But how could I trust myself and my choices? I mean, it had not served me so far. At this point, I lost my excellent credit, all my money, most of my belongings, my friends, my family, my relationships and soon my house. I felt alone, and for the first time, I was really starting to doubt myself. After all the hurtful things that were said and done to me throughout my lifetime, I have always been able to find a way to make it through. I was like a phoenix always resurrecting from the ashes. I had incredible determination and I was told that I had the patience of a saint. I personally do not know anyone who has the strength I do. It surprised everyone, including myself.

No one was ever able to completely knock me down, or completely get under my skin. I have been able to prevail so many times that it became an automatic response. But this time, I was completely worn down and it actually started to scare me. I was the only person who I could truly count on. What was I to do now? I had endured chronic stress for well over a year. I was completely malnourished and underweight. I started to feel depressed, guilty, regretful, and hopeless. I was knocked down one too many times…I was down for the count.

Then my daughter, Jasmine came into my room and blurted out, "Auntie Stacy sure loves bashing you!" It's funny, how a mother can find strength when they need to protect their children. I got up out of bed and went to Jasmine's room to see what she was talking to me about. There on her computer, she showed me an e-mail.

NOTE TO SELF: EMPOWERMENT

Date: Sat, 13 Dec 2008 15:01:40 -0800
From: Stacy (name and e-mail address deleted for privacy)
Subject: Miss you...
To: Jasmine

Hi sunshine! Just writing to see when I can take you and Brooklyn shopping and see you. I noticed your mom took you and Brooklyn off my friends list for Facebook. That's sad. I don't know why she's deciding to be mad again when all I ever do is try to help her. I should be the one who is mad at her but I try to be understanding and patient with her. I don't know what she is telling you but she tells her business partner and Auntie Sassa that I never call her. I looked through my phone bills and I have called her 8 times over the last couple of months and she has not once called me back. I should forward my phone bills to them so that she would stop lying. She said that I don't talk to you girls but has decided to take you off my Facebook to keep me from talking to you. I don't think I'll ever understand her. The main thing is that I love you girls and don't want to be kept from you. It's not fair. Your mom has her issues and it makes her feel better to blame me for her problems and I am okay with that. Whatever makes her feel better. I hate that it has to be that way but it makes things easier on her to blame me instead of taking

ownership of her problems. Hopefully one day she will grow up and stop mistreating people who care about her and stop trying so hard to please people who only use her. I know that my life has been really busy since I was forced to sell the business and return to school but no matter how busy I am, I will always be there for you girls. If you need to talk or need a place to stay, I am there for you and Brooklyn. Your mom has decided she never wants to talk to me........again....but, she is another story. I can't save her. Believe me, I have tried. I wish that I could make everything easier for her but somehow she likes the crisis and drama and that's just not for me. I like things to be simple, to enjoy life and the precious time with family. I really hope to see you before Christmas. I love you very much and am always thinking of you and Brooklyn. You are truly two wonderful girls and have done a great job at raising yourselves. I love you to pieces and miss you so much.
Talk to you soon.
Hugs and kisses.

Auntie Stacy
xoxoxo

On December 13th no less. This date is the anniversary of my mother's death. That is really twisting the knife in my heart. My sister and I can dispute until the end of time over the details of the business. I am comfortable knowing what the truth is. One thing is for sure...I am NOT a liar.

I have reached a point where I no longer feel that I need to defend myself. The truth speaks for itself. I also learned that *actions speak louder than words*. Although I had lost all my money through this bad business decision, in the big picture, that did not matter to me. Money comes and goes and there are more important things to me than money. Where was my sister? She claimed to have loved me, but where was the love?

What type of sister goes to their niece and bashes their mother? Children look up to their mother. Why would anyone shatter that? I have always been an amazing mother. That is one thing I knew I did right. Meet my two girls and it would be a true testament to that. I was angry and could have retaliated by spreading some nasty truths about my sister, but I didn't. I am proud of myself for that.

I could handle her saying things to my best friend/business partner, my grandfather, my family and my ex-husband. But going to my daughter...that was a low blow. Talk about kicking someone while they are down. Just when I thought that this was all she could do to try and hurt me...there was always more. As she expressed in the e-mail, she had offered only Jasmine and Brooklyn a place to stay. Where would that leave me?

I noticed a change in Jasmine's behavior towards me. I felt that she was becoming more and more distant. My intuition was telling me that my sister was filling her head with things, but I refused to believe it because I had other issues to deal with. At the time, I had cut my sister out of my life. I still allowed her to be a part of my girls' life, even though she wasn't the greatest towards me.

Do not ignore your intuition! It turned out, I was right. My daughter, Jasmine later admitted that she was starting to believe all the horrible things that her aunt was constantly saying about me. I am sure that I was not at my best during that time, but I was not a bad mother.

You may feel bad for thinking horrible things about people, but if you continually have a nagging feeling, your intuition is trying to tell you something. I remember Wayne Dyer saying, *"If your prayers are you talking to God, then your intuition is God talking to you"*.

Thankfully, my sister Lisa and brother-in-law Kevin allowed Jasmine, Brooklyn and I to stay at their house for a few months. We were to have a small corner in their cold, unfinished basement with cement walls and floors. We did not care, since my two girls and I would not have to live on the streets. I was extremely grateful that we would have a safe place to stay, with people we could count on to not hurt us. It would also soften the blow from us losing everything, to be around loving, family members.

They offered us to stay free of charge. I would not take advantage of this, by promising Lisa that we would only stay there for four months. That would give me enough time to get back on my feet. I had a big ship to turn around. I had four months to get a job, put myself back together and build strength after that hard hit. I would have to save up enough for first and last month's rent. I also needed to find an apartment close to both of my girls' schools, that would accept tenants with bad credit and a new job. Wow, that part bothered me because I had always had excellent credit. I had a lot to tackle.

The hardest thing that I was forced to lose was my dignity and pride. I had to learn to become humble and to simplify. And boy did I simplify. This turned out to be my greatest lesson and greatest gift. I was focusing too hard on my outward appearances that the Universe forced me to look at what truly mattered in life.

The only thing I had on my side, was the truth. I had gained awareness and was also blessed with the gift of discernment. Now that the true colors and truths were exposed, I would no longer be playing the role of the fool. I also felt that I would be able to make more informed decisions and healthier choices with these new tools.

There was no denying the truth, and I felt some power in knowing it. I knew things would be different this time, because I felt different. I started to trust myself again and I no longer felt lifeless. The power within me started to stir and flourish.

This was all new territory for me and I felt like this may be the turning point in my life. Naturally, I wondered how this time things would be different. But since I was now down to my core being, I trusted myself. I had a deep understanding of my past choices, behavior and patterns. I also recognized the patterns of others and was determined to break this vicious cycle.

It turned out that I had become like my mother. Although I love her dearly, I definitely inherited her poor choices. I was determined not to pass that down to my two girls. I was tired of the life I was living and I no longer had the tolerance for people treating me poorly. I began to realize that I have a choice. *I cannot control what others do to me, but I can control my own actions and how much that I will or will not put up with.*

I felt strongly compelled to make a final attempt at redeeming my father-daughter relationship. I was prepared this time for another disappointment, but I had to try the best I could. I have to take responsibility for my own actions. I am the one who has to live with myself and my choices. If I felt that there was something more I could do on my end, I needed to trust myself, so I would have no regrets.

I felt that my father did not have a clear understanding of who I was or how I felt. I thought if I brought him up to speed, then we could put the past behind us and move forward into the future. This e-mail is fast-forwarding us quite a few years, but I told you, it took me a long time to learn. I am including this in this chapter, to hopefully shorten your learning curve and ease your pain.

This is the actual e-mail that I copied and pasted. I corrected a few spelling mistakes to make it easier to read. I stated in the e-mail that my younger sister was 20 years old, but need to clarify that it is an approximate age, as I was not sure of the exact one. I also removed some names and content, solely to protect my father and his second family. From what I have seen, he is an amazing husband and father to them and I would not want to destroy this.

NOTE TO SELF: EMPOWERMENT

Subject: I love you. Good thing you are retired...you will need a lot of time to read this!
From: Trina
Date: Sun, 1 Sep 2013 13:58:59 -0400
To: Dad

Good Morning Dad!

First thing I want to say is I am not mad at you. With that being said, please be patient with me as I feel I need to catch you up to speed, so you can understand me better. I need to express how I feel and my perspective in hopes to establish a relationship between us free of misunderstandings and unhealed wounds.

I am very happy that you have met Sofia and I have two additional sisters who are amazing. Compiled on to the feeling of never being good enough for you, skinny enough, abandoned etc...I often feel that you had a "fresh start" with your new family and have wiped clean from your old family until recently.

Dad, your first born child is now 41 years old and you truly have no clue who I am or much of anything I have been through, accomplished, feel...really anything. What woke me up to that fact is if you were serious and genuine when you asked me about what happened to the house I had FOUR YEARS AGO!

We will get to that later, but first I need to really tell you about my entire life and how I feel. It may feel like I am dishing out the past, but in our case/relationship I feel it is a last attempt for me to try and have any type of authentic relationship with you.

Instead of going through missed milestones in mine and your grandchildren's lives (one who is already an adult now), I am going to try and keep focused on things that affect just you and I. Things that took part in shaping me and still in some way affect my life today. I am going to be completely honest of my perspective - in hopes that we can work through this. I need to be completely honest as this will be the fastest road to healing our relationship.

From the day I was born, I felt I was a disappointment and never good enough for you. From the moment I came into this world and it was announced "It's A Girl!" You have repeatedly made it known to me that you wanted a boy! I understand you felt pressure as you were the last one to carry on the name. If it makes you feel better...my last name is still "Hall".

As it turned out, the first part of my childhood I was a "tomboy". When my friends were outside playing, I was with you and your stopwatch. You would time me as I would run around the block and then make me do it again, and sometimes again, to try and improve my time. Most of my memories are of being forced to run and play basketball.

My last day of being forced to run was the summer before 8th Grade when I almost died. (It may have been before 7th grade, but I remember it was before entering middle school. I added this for clarification.) You had forced me to run every race, be in every event (long jump, standing long jump, high jump etc.) in as many different age categories as I was eligible to be in. It was a hot, July summers day at The Fireman's Track Meet in Timmins. I didn't really have much break between all the events, much less was I given water or even an orange.

Immediately after the track meet, we all got in the car to drive to North Bay to see Grandma Hall's new house. I was throwing up the whole ride there and didn't even (still to this day) get to see her house as I went straight to bed and was vomiting the whole night. I continued vomiting throughout 2 more entire days. It was grandma who would periodically checked on me and give me ginger ale and Gravol, but nothing would stay down. It was on the 3rd night that I could hear Grandma say to you "If she throws up one more time, we are bringing her to the hospital!"

Shortly thereafter, there I was lying on a stretcher with a doctor saying over me...this part I remember as if it was yesterday: "You are very lucky you brought her in...another half hour and you she may have died."

I was not happy. I was severely dehydrated. Although I was so extremely weak at that time, the shock of those words woke me up. I was on intravenous for days and then gradually progressed to being able to have only soup broth, Popsicles and Jello. I was not allowed to get out of my bed. I couldn't walk to a pay phone to call my mother. I had to be pushed around in a wheelchair because I could not afford to exert even a small amount of energy! That was really hard for me to understand as a child. Did the doctors not know that I wiped out almost every 1st place ribbon??? I was young and supposed to be out playing, not be laying in a hospital bed and using wheelchairs?!?!

When I got out of the hospital our stay with Grandma was already over and I just had to say goodbye.

I know we already touched on this upcoming topic before, but I feel compelled to write everything all together in ONE e-mail. It is a lot, but at least it is altogether and can be easy to be re-read if it is too much to be absorbed all at once. It is important to have the entire picture of me instead of little snapshots.

NOTE TO SELF: EMPOWERMENT

I was in continuous fear of you as a child and was constantly walking on eggshells trying not to set you off. I understand back in those days, it was much more common and acceptable to use a belt. I felt that I was always making you angry and often getting the belt. Sometimes those bouts would seem to go on for a long time. I remember the exact moment while you were hitting me that I learned to mentally block out any pain and was not afraid of you or anyone!

The worst was the verbal attacks. You would always comment on my weight. I would constantly feel like I was fat. This still affects me to this day. I have a distorted self-image. I still feel like I am fat and at this exact moment I am writing this. Even if other people are telling me the complete opposite.

So to sum up the 13 years I spent with you as a child, were not the greatest. You were often arguing with my mother.

One memory that stands out is when we lived in Gold Centre. I was locked in the room with my crying and scared mother. She had pulled the green dresser over the door and we were sitting in front of it, while you were continually banging on the door full force. All the while, I felt helpless watching my mother completely scared and upset. I was trying to console her to the sound of your banging. You banged so hard, that eventually you broke the mirror on the dresser. I remember saying, "Don't worry mom, he'll have 7 Years bad luck!" She actually laughed and I felt good that I could bring her some relief...even if was for a moment. It was really hard to be in between this. I love my mom so much. She was the one who was constantly there for me. I know that there are 2 sides and she may have not been perfect, but the one fact remains...she was ALWAYS there for me and she always showed me that she loves me...so whose side would you take? Plus I had experienced much of the same pain from you, which would make her more credible.

Then you are off to Mexico. You and grandma often blamed my mother and us girls for not writing you letters. When really let's look at it. I was 13...What girl at that age is thinking of writing letters??? Plus...let's really look at it realistically. You could put all the blame on whomever you wish, but when it really comes down to it...you were the adult and you were the parent. I never ever received a phone call on my birthday (still to this day...by the way I was born on January 3rd) or a letter for that matter. I can tell you this much...there is no way in hell that I would ever do that to any one of my kids. If Jasmine got busy at school, life or her boyfriend...there is no way I would blame her for not calling or writing. (And she is an adult now and is able to make better decisions...also technology is much more advanced and easier to access people through e-mail, text, FaceTime, Skype etc.). I would make every effort as a parent to keep in touch with my kids. As a parent, my relationship with my children are my #1 priority! They always have been and always will be. I know you were provided much misinformation, but the beauty of it all is, I do not have to waste my time having to defend myself as a mother. Just spend some time with my girls and that's the true testament. There is a reason Kevin stopped me in the driveway last Sunday at Stacy's just to make sure he commented on how great my girls are. He proceeded to say "You should teach a class; I'd take it!"

So here I am, an extremely insecure child being raised by a single mom. In my own little way I became rebellious. I no longer would run or play basketball and would do the most girlish things possible and took up dancing from Grade 4-8. You would even put me down about that. Saying, "Why are you taking dancing? The only way you can use that is if you become a Stripper".

Then I got shipped off to Mexico in Grade 11. She told me, "If you don't want any rules, go live with your dad." I said "Ok" calling her bluff which I thought she was doing. What was going through my head is that there is no way she would send me off to live with you. But she did!

Four years later, when I was 20 years old, I won $5000. One of the first things I wanted to do besides paying off my student loan was go back to Mexico to visit you. I was so excited that I finally had a bit of extra money! It was a long 4 years...I just wanted to go back!!!!

We arranged to meet in Melaque, as we spent a lot of time there together and had many happy memories. I had to fly to Manzanillo and try and find a way to Melaque on my own. It was a Friday and you were to meet me as soon as you could after school. I got a hotel room where we would always stay and it was going to be like "old times"!! I stayed there by myself the whole entire weekend and you never showed up. I would spend the day on the beach and then hide out alone in the hotel room. My old friends would be banging on the door at night for "Disco Trina" to come out but I was wiser and was not going to be the blonde going out alone in Mexico.

For whatever reason you did not come meet me and then I had to find my way own way to Guadalajara (If I knew you were going to do that to me, I would have just flown to Guadalajara).

I befriended a girl that worked at the Hotel and we took a bus together back to Manzanillo and she let me stay at her house until a bus to Guadalajara came. (I don't know what I would have done without her as I had no clue where to go and my Spanish wasn't as good as it was 4 years prior).

I finally made it to Guadalajara at 11-11:30 at night. I rushed to call you to come pick me up. You said, "You have two options...you can take a cab..." I stopped you right there. Were you for real???? You left me stranded for the weekend in Melaque having to dish out more money than expected for hotel, buses etc. and now you weren't even going to pick me up?? You wanted me to take a taxi in a huge city, in a country I am not even from, to your place? You didn't even live on Entre Rios anymore!!! I didn't even know where you lived...but you wanted me to somehow get there and expect a taxi driver who doesn't even speak English to get me there???? There were not two options.....You came to pick me up. The week went by and you barely spent time with me but you did keep up the tradition of bringing me to Guadalajara Grill the night before I left apologizing to me for not spending that much time with me.

Surprising I still kept in touch with you and made plans to spend my own money to come see you again a few years later. I was excited about you meeting your first grandchild. Unfortunately Jasmine was not able to come last minute because of documents needed. I had no way of contacting you to tell you. I was debating not going but didn't want to waste your time and keep you waiting at the airport wondering...so I made a quick decision and rearrangements and went on my own. I got to see my two half-sisters, but again no memorable moments with you except our final night at Guadalajara Grill.

For the 3rd time, I made a decision to go visit you. Jasmine and I spent Christmas on the year Jasmine turned 2. You, Sofia, my two half-sisters, Jasmine and I all stayed at a really nice resort in Nuevo Vallarta. You got us joining rooms. You thought it would be a good idea for you and your family stay together and Jasmine and I stay in a separate room. You said that we could come in the morning through the joining door and we could have breakfast together. Each and every morning, your part of the adjoining room would be locked and Jasmine and I could never go in your room. Jasmine and I would just spend much of the morning just her and I. By this time I already felt like you had two SEPARATE families, but this trip really reinforced that fact.

Once e-mail was invented...I would keep in touch with you more often, but one thing is for sure... I NEVER missed your birthday. I would always e-mail you or call you if you were living in Niagara Falls or Bowmanville. I was the one who would go with my girls and visit you in Niagara Falls and Bowmanville. I was the one throughout all those years that would invite you over to my house or meet up with you at Yorkdale Mall. Stacy and Lisa refused to come

NOTE TO SELF: EMPOWERMENT

and I was the one who always made the effort. Be patient...all what I'm saying now will tie in and hopefully make some sense to you.

Unfortunately, I have to spend my day off writing this e-mail just to catch you up to speed. I'm doing this because I care. My mom always said, "It's a lot easier to not care than to care." She is right. I could easily just not write this and go on with my life.

So...we are finally getting to last Sunday. You are bringing up Europe which in my head is bringing up empty promises and disappointment brought on by you in the past. At this point I am not really bothered, just trying to understand what is going on???

This was the final blow!!! You asked me where I was living. Am I in an apartment? A house? Am I renting? Do I own? This is a legit question. I let you know that we are in a house...but renting. Then you asked..."What ever happened to that other house?" I was kind of thrown back a bit. You couldn't possible mean the house I owned for 9 years??? So I asked you again..."which house"? Yep....you meant THAT house!!!!!

You got to be kidding me???? You are bringing all this up now at a family gathering...after the Europe blow??? After FOUR years have gone by??? You are concerned NOW after ALL that?!?! I thought you were joking, but when I could clearly see you were serious, I answered your question in front of everyone in hopes to trigger your memory and put this conversation to a halt. I told you that "I lost everything." Then you proceeded to say "Oh, in the divorce?"

That was it!!!! I was checked out right there!! You really have absolutely no clue or have been fed so much misinformation. Something!! I said "No, because of the whole Stacy and business thing. By your look I could tell it sparked some sort of memory, but I know now that you have no clue what has or is going on with me.

I got the house June 28th, 2001. My mother passed away December 13, 2000 and left us 3 money and we all used it different ways. I chose to buy a house. I was married at the time so it was both of our house.

We separated November 9th, 2003. So basically 2 Years later. We did all the settlements and I gave him some money, but now the house was mine.

I owned it ON MY OWN for SIX MORE YEARS!!!! So in absolutely NO WAY did it have to do with the divorce to answer that question. I WORKED really hard ON MY OWN...no husband, no boyfriend or no roommate helping! Pretty impressive huh? I was a single mom, doing an amazing job raising two

NOTE TO SELF: EMPOWERMENT

amazing girls and paying for all their lessons etc. on her own.

SIX YEARS! There was only one period of time understandably that set me back a little. It was after the divorce and I already told you that I was drugged and raped. This really messed with my head, so it was hard to function at my best during that time. You helped me out and gave me $1000. Thank you so much! It was hard to tell you but I did, and you helped. That was all I needed to put me back on track. Stacy helped me with $300 for hydro once and that is it in the ENTIRE SIX YEARS. Stacy was at the hospital with me the entire day/evening just after I was raped. It was my boss at State Farm that called the State Farm Stacy worked at because she was extremely worried about me.

I really had a hard struggle emotionally during that time, but I didn't let myself break down and continued to work and pay for the bills and the house on my own for MANY more years to come.

Stacy was rushing to sell the business. During this time financially I was still in a really good position. I had lots of equity in my house and all my bills were getting paid.

I am not going to rehash all the stuff about the business and Stacy because I already sent you that e-mail FOUR YEARS AGO as a DESPERATE PLEA FOR HELP TO YOU!!!!

When I needed to BORROW $10,000 to save the house I got the insane idea to go to my father. I have seen it on tv and movies that fathers would do anything for their little girls. I would have paid you back. I knew writing the e-mail to you was a longshot. In all honesty, I really wasn't expecting you to come through for me, but it was more a test. If I, someone who has done everything on her own needs desperate help...would my father step in when it mattered most? Would he help his first born child and his two grandchildren who are under chronic, unhealthy stress?? Who are frightened they would have absolutely no place to go and are barely eating??? Hmm... Would be interesting? Let's see??

My response from you..."I am CHOOSING not to help you." That was harsh to hear from my own father. It was the 2nd time in my ENTIRE life that I ever asked you for any help of any kind. You said that I needed to learn "how to fish". That part right there proves you don't even know your own daughter. People who "really" know me, think I am the STRONGEST person ever!!! I already responded to that, but it's important that you know that I KNOW how to fish!!!! I honestly can say that I have been fishing my ENTIRE life. Trust me when I say that you weren't helping me in the very least when you CHOSE not to help me and your two granddaughters. We needed you to just give us a break and feed us a fish, so I could get enough strength and energy to go back out fishing. This is what I do best because it is the only thing I know I can say I'm an expert at doing. That was fine if you were choosing not to LEND us the money. You also had a house in Bowmanville that later I find out you have your 20 year old daughter living in by herself. As your daughter, how am I supposed to feel about that?? Besides the money or the house...most importantly where was the loving, fatherly concern? You are telling me it took you FOUR YEARS to finally care what happened to Jasmine, Brooklyn and I??? Also you happened to mention that you have not heard from me and I only ask for money". This part I just love..."Stacy is making a RECENT AND SINCERE effort with you".

Wow!!!! What do I say to that? In the 1 1/2 years I was struggling and under chronic stress, I was trying to conserve enough energy to put on a brave face for my girls and trying to keep all 3 of us surviving!!!

In the meantime, I have my dear sister Stacy go to EVERYONE while I am knocked down and have no energy to defend myself and tries to completely take away my support system!!! TALK ABOUT KICKING SOMEONE WHO IS DOWN!!!

You are telling me it's sincere when after ALL these years she starts talking to you? I was the one there throughout all these years (all the things I mentioned earlier). Then when I'm down for a little bit all those efforts are meaningless??? You mean I could have saved all that money and time and DECADES I spent making an effort with you and just could have made an effort now and look like the hero?

I KNOW who I can count on. I know who truly loves me and cares about my well-being and has my best interests at heart. I love how my life is now and the people I have close to me.

I wasn't intending for this e-mail to be so long, but I guess it's pretty good for 41 years of catching up on. Obviously I still care, otherwise I would not spend 6 hours writing this. A father does have a great influence on a daughter's life whether he was in it or not. I guess I was given these tools so I could help my daughter, Brooklyn who is going through the same thing. Never feeling loved or good enough for her father.

Thank you for reading this e-mail. I understand that some of this must be difficult to read. Let me know if you want to talk about anything.

    Love Trina

After spending over 6 hours on my only day off to write this e-mail, this is the response I got...

NOTE TO SELF: EMPOWERMENT

From: Dad
To: Trina
CC: Dad
Subject: RE: I love you. Good thing you are retired...you will need a lot of time to read this!
Date: Sun, 1 Sep 2013 15:04:12 -0400

Good Afternoon Trina

I KNOW who I can count on. I know who truly loves me and cares about my well-being and has my best interests at heart. I love how my life is now and the people I have close to me.

I am sure the above applies to both of us.

Take care.
Dad

Wow! That was his effort after pouring out my heart and soul? This is my father's response in its entirety. There is absolutely no editing or deleting. My father did not even take the time to write a response. Most of his reply was him copying and pasting a portion of my e-mail. It is funny that from all that I have written, that is what he got from it. Why do I continually feel a need to put myself through this? See my point, how there is nothing that you can say or do that is right with certain people? It's best to let it go and find people who truly appreciate how magnificent you are.

TRUST YOURSELF

You did the work in the last chapter. You wrote down your truths. Knowing the truth will help you make decisions accordingly and not based on lies. You now have a deeper understanding of where you are and what you need to deal with. You survived! It is going to get even better.

Trusting yourself is the key to your happiness. It seems simple enough, but how do you trust yourself, when you have a history of making bad choices? Or when people have put negative thoughts into your head, which have resulted in self-doubt? Even if you have removed yourself from these people, the emotional scars and residual negative effects still remain. You may feel like you are not good enough, smart enough or just feel stuck. It is natural to wonder if you are doing the right thing. You may lose trust in others and also yourself.

I was continually getting it wrong in regards to choosing a partner. I had close family and friends knocking me down and kicking me while I was down. My life was surrounded by drama and hurtful people. Intellectually, I knew it was wrong, but it was familiar to me. Sadly, it was the only way that I have ever known.

Eventually, I reached a point, where I gathered enough inner strength to know that I deserved better. I struggled with trusting myself to make healthy and right decisions. This was a tough reality and a long process. I would like to share the lessons I have learned to help fast track you to complete happiness and to believing in yourself.

STOP LISTENING TO CONDITIONED AND NEGATIVE SELF-TALK

These are voices of your parents, siblings, or anyone who has made you feel like you are not worthy or good enough. Listen to positive affirmations to help replace all this negativity. Slowly, but surely, you will begin to get stronger and trust your own inner voice.

SURROUND YOURSELF WITH POSITIVE PEOPLE

Positive people allow you to be who you truly are and will love you unconditionally. They create a safe environment for you to be authentic and live your life the way you are meant to. You will feel appreciated and valued, which will help you trust that you are doing the right thing.

OVERCOME YOUR FEAR OF THE UNKNOWN

When you take risks and stay true to yourself, your whole world opens up. When you conquer your fears, it boosts your confidence.

TRUST YOUR INTUITION

You hear people saying all the time to "follow your intuition" or "go with your gut feeling". How many times have you gone against your gut, only to be wrong and say, "I knew I should have" or "I knew it all along"? It is extremely important to listen to your inner voice and wisdom. This is your deep "knowing". Trust this to guide you along the right path, which leads you to happiness.

DO WHAT YOU FEEL YOU NEED TO DO

Do not worry about what others will think or say. If you need to say something...say it. If you want to do something...do it. Do not hold back and you will never have to wonder what if...

BE AUTHENTIC

You do not have to defend yourself to people who truly *know* you and *get* you. That is such a wonderful feeling. You do not even need to say a word. They can see things for what they are. You can just relax and be yourself, while being loved unconditionally. It is that simple. You no longer have to explain yourself to people who are committed to misunderstanding you. That is a waste of your time and energy, because you will never be able to please them. You will never be good enough for them. This only makes you feel worse about yourself.

    We are trying to build you up and gain trust in who you are. People should like you, for you. You are not such a horrible person. We are all human, each learning and growing. We make mistakes. As long as we are doing things with honest intentions and a pure heart, how horrible could we be? Give yourself some slack. When living life with these morals, there is nothing that you can do that is unforgivable. Trust this in you.

    It does not matter what the jealous people say about you. They may only be able to fool people short-term.

Eventually, their true colors will show and people will be able to figure out the truth for themselves.

It all boils down to fully trusting and believing in yourself. Do not doubt yourself. You took ample time to make these huge strides forward, so do not turn back now. Just do what you feel is right. If your intentions are good, then what more can you ask for? You are doing the best you can. Trust your inner voice, stay true to yourself, and be happy!

5

STEP 3: REMOVE TOXIC PEOPLE

Days before my girls and I were about to move, my sister Lisa called me and expressed a deep concern. She was talking to Stacy, who warned her if we got into a fight by me living there, that I would cut her out of my life. Lisa did not want this and started to have doubts. She was seriously considering not allowing us to live with her. I cannot believe that my sister went to the only person who offered us a place to stay!

    I could understand Lisa's concern, as I was cutting toxic people out of my life, right, left and center. But this would not happen with Lisa. I did not appreciate the newly found doubts in Lisa's mind, which almost prevented her from helping us when we were in dire need.

    As I became more and more frustrated with people, it became much easier to cut out the toxic people. I was running out of patience with them. I was also valuing myself and did not feel like I deserved to be treated poorly anymore.

I was already losing everything, and I figured this would be a fresh start. I pulled out a piece of paper and made 3 columns. One saying "Safe People", 2nd with the heading "Maybe" and the last column "Toxic People". I had decided that I would only be allowing the "Safe People" into my life. The "Maybe" column still had a chance to make its way into my "new" life, but they only had until my moving date to cross over. Once I was out of my house, my new life would begin. I was only going to bring the loving and encouraging people along with me.

After this process, there were not very many people whom I was going to allow into my new life. I did not care. All I cared about was building my life back up for me and my girls. We had been through enough, and I was not going to allow any more needless suffering. People have now shown me their true colors. Maya Angelou said "When people show you their true colors, believe them the first time." I refused to do this before, but I know better now. I have no more excuses.

As I surrounded myself with only safe people and cut out the toxic ones, I started to feel better about myself. These people were not putting me down and they gave me the freedom to be myself. I could talk to them, without having to worry about what I said being used against me, or spread around town. I started to love myself more and also started to accept myself. I realized that I was not such a horrible person and that I actually had a kind and loving heart.

It was one of my closest friends who helped me to see this. Mandy has known me since I was 18 years old. She knew me from my very first boyfriend, before my marriage, before my children and before my mother's terminal illness. She has seen me go through most of my life. If any friend knows me the most, it would be Mandy.

One day, during a phone conversation, Mandy kept going on about how perfect I was. She could not stop saying kind things about me. This got me thinking. Here is a person who has known me for over 20 years and she is saying *I am perfect*? She knows all of my bad choices. She has watched me go through all that I have gone through and she could not even say one bad word about me?

Then why was I listening to all of these other people, who did not really know me or were not out for my best interests? Why was I putting so much value on their opinions? My two closest and longest friends, Mandy and Kimberley, were not talking to me that way? In fact, in over 20 years, they were only saying amazing things about me. How did the toxic people manage to move to the forefront of my life, when amazing people like Mandy and Kimberley got overshadowed? I decided that these should be the people who I should be listening to, as they knew me the best.

I removed all the people who were hurting me and making me feel like I was worthless. It did not matter if they were my sister, father or grandfather. Simply being a family member of mine, no longer carried any weight with me. It did not matter if we had blood ties, they should not be treating me like crap. They are supposed to love me, nurture me and encourage me. It is one thing to not care about me and leave me alone. I would have been fine with that, but I could no longer take the verbal put-downs. Since I have done nothing to warrant this type of treatment, I would settle for nothing less.

You grew up hearing that "blood is thicker than water", but how long do you need to feel obligated to tolerate negative and corrosive behavior, on the sole fact that they are your family? What do you do when you are in this situation? This is tough. You need to think long and hard about it. How much of their behavior you continue to allow or accept is completely up to you.

Having one toxic person in your life can easily turn your life into a downward spiral. They are like a poison that seeps under your skin. Their negativity will eventually start to get to you and before you know if, you may turn into a person who you no longer recognize. It will start weighing you down.

I understand how difficult it is to remove a toxic person out of your life. They do not make it easy for you. They use manipulation and guilt to keep you from leaving or thinking clearly. Many times there are more than one of these negative people in your life. They are often the people closest to you and can be your parent, sibling, friend, partner, or co-worker. I was surrounded by them at one point of my life. I was not able to see clearly during that time and did not realize that this was my reality. A toxic person did not even phase me, since that was my normal way of life. Only once I started to eliminate each and every harmful person out of my life...did my life finally change for the better. I now have zero tolerance for a poisonous person, as I understand the havoc they cause. It also fuels this passion within me to prevent others from experiencing the same pain and downfall.

Now that you know your truths and trust yourself, you have a solid foundation to work with. Do not waver from this, or you will find yourself regressing. You have made it this far, let's push through this together. Your life will be so much better on the other side. You will get to the point of no return and you will not have to deal with these struggles again. You will feel so powerful and you will become an unstoppable force.

It is important that you connect to your inner wisdom and what you already know. Reference your answers from the last chapter, to ensure that you do not sway from who you are. We are closer to discovering the real you. *Your inner voice will grow stronger than all of the outer voices.* We want this. Let's break through any old negative beliefs. You have been conditioned for many years and it will take some effort on your part to disrupt negative patterns.

Some people make a clean sweep. They had enough and are not going to put up with it any longer. You will wonder how you were able to tolerate it for so long. Others find this a difficult process. Once you see the benefits of removing a negative person, you will begin to not like hearing the insults and criticism. You will have more time for the encouraging and positive people. Your confidence will build and so will your inner power. You will no longer have that person destroying your progress along the way. The toxic people keep you at bay, so you do not have the strength to stand up to them. It takes a lot of energy to stand up to these people and not back down.

They sense how powerful you are within, and they are insecure.

There are plenty of people out there who will love you unconditionally. They will encourage you, support you and uplift you. You need to distance yourself from the toxic people in your life in order to make room for these amazing people. No one wants to come to terms with the fact that someone close to you may be hurting you the most. I love you enough to help you recognize the truth, so you can start taking steps towards healthier choices and relationships.

10 WAYS TO RECOGNIZE A TOXIC PERSON IN YOUR LIFE

1. Only calls you when they want or need something. They rarely call to see how you are doing, unless they are bored and have nothing better to do.
2. Will not give you space when you need it. A toxic person is afraid to give you space because you may have time to think and come to your senses.
3. Are not happy when you are happy. They often seem jealous and make you feel bad when you share great news. You start to feel as though you are bragging and that you can no longer share the extraordinary moments in your life.
4. Does not encourage or support you. In fact, a toxic person often sabotages your life.
5. Makes it extremely difficult to say no to them. They use manipulation and guilt to make you feel bad.
6. You cannot count on them. They are not there when you need them, but you better always be

there for them! They will only be there for you if it benefits them or they have absolutely no other plans.
7. You feel drained after being with them or talking to them. A toxic person often takes advantage of you and also takes you for granted. They take an overwhelming amount of your energy, time and money, without much reciprocation.
8. Plays games with your emotions and heart. They often lure you in with their charm, but then push you away with negative comments and insults.
9. Makes you feel like you are always walking on eggshells. Nothing you do seems right or good enough. They get angry and have a short fuse with you...especially if you call them out on something they are doing wrong. They love to turn the blame around on you.
10. They make you feel bad when you spend time with other people. They do not want you to listen to family or friends, who genuinely care about you and may speak the truth about their poor behavior. They are demanding of your time and make you feel that you should only have time for them.

The people who you surround yourself with, can make or break you. Some people can drain you, use you, or constantly put you down. Others can make you feel like you can never do anything right, no matter how hard you try. You may find yourself in a constant battle, trying to please others, leaving you depleted and unhappy in the process. You do not have to tolerate this. You have a choice.

Toxic people can have a pattern of negatively impacting your life. It can be damaging and very unhealthy for your well-being. Do not hold on to them because they have become a part of your routine and are familiar to you. Do not be afraid to let go of the things or people which no longer serve your higher good. If it is weighing you down and preventing you from your full potential...let it go.

If someone handed you a spoonful of a poisonous liquid, you wouldn't jump at the chance to drink it, would you? Yet we find ourselves more tolerant with poisonous people. It is imperative that you protect yourself when it comes to people as well. You will have to make some difficult decisions, but in the end it will lead to a happier and more peaceful life.

Poisonous people can seep under your skin and leave you feeling sick and terrible inside. It can be extremely damaging to your self-worth. This may be a harsh reality, but often these toxic people are the ones closest to you. Because they are so close, you may find yourself being much more accepting and more likely to justify their negative behavior.

FAMILY

Parents, siblings or any family member can be extremely toxic. They are your family. They are supposed to unconditionally love you and support you. Many times family members can be the most damaging; especially when it is a parent.

FRIENDS

Friends can be draining. Some often suck you into their drama. You may feel obligated to listen to them and also try to save them. You think you are helping them, but you really aren't. You give them advice, but they never take it. Some can be selfish and you need to revolve your life around them. You are always there for them, but the one time you need them, they are nowhere to be found. Does this sound familiar?

CO-WORKERS

In most workplaces, you may come across at least one person that is always complaining and is negative. You come to work in a great mood, and within minutes of being around this person, you may feel a shift in the entire work atmosphere. This person may point out every little mistake you make and is the first to make it known. You know the type.

It is important to take some serious time to think about these people in your life. These are the people who are resulting in you having a good day or a bad day. These are the people who are contributing to the majority of your stress or happiness. The choice is yours.

LOVE YOURSELF ENOUGH TO LET THESE TOXIC PEOPLE GO

SOME TOXIC PEOPLE WILL LET YOU GO WITH EASE

As soon as you are no longer tolerating the way they treat you or have discovered their true colors, they dismiss you like everything you ever had together meant absolutely nothing. This can hurt. You have put in so much time and effort into loving, helping and supporting them, only to find out that your relationship carries no weight? You point out their behavior and they hold no accountability. Instead they use this tactic, which somehow turns things onto you. I have seen those games played, way too many times. When they realize that you have "figured" them out, they are gone...just like that. It does not make sense, but let them go. They do not value the relationship as much as you do. You deserve better!

SOME TOXIC PEOPLE WILL MAKE IT DIFFICULT TO LET THEM GO

These people have something to lose by you moving forward without them. You offer them something that they do not want to give up. Also, you moving on without them in pursuit of your happiness and well-being, may pose a threat to their insecurities.

SOME TOXIC PEOPLE YOU CANNOT AVOID IN YOUR LIFE

Sometimes you just cannot get away from some of these toxic people. You want to remove them out of your life, but they are at your workplace, or keep showing up at a social gathering or family events. In these situations, it is important to set boundaries. You need to set your limits to what you are willing to accept or tolerate. If they cross the line, remove yourself and walk away. Find a happy, positive and loving person instead to be around.

LETTING GO

Letting go is extremely difficult, and is easier said than done. Many people have trouble letting go, especially when there is emotional pain or disappointment. You get "stuck". There is a heavy weight from the past that you continue to carry, making it challenging to move forward.

I had a private message from a friend, asking me how I went about letting go of the past. This dear friend cannot stop thinking about a certain person. These thoughts bring about nothing but negative emotions, but still he continues to torture himself. You may have someone in your life who continually brings up past issues that make it more difficult to move on and be completely happy. You are not alone if you or someone close to you is having trouble letting go.

People are at different stages throughout this journey. Many people can remain stagnant for years. I know because I have been there. People would spend countless hours giving me uplifting talks and reasons to move forward, but I would still be in the exact same place. It makes sense why there are so many people talking or writing books, songs and movies about letting go. No matter how many people talk about this untimely topic, ultimately the work is up to you. When you are ready and have had enough, you will let go of your past for good. With me, I heard the same thing a thousand times, but then one day, I finally got it! Hopefully, this message is received at the right time or in just the right way that you need to hear it.

DO PEOPLE EVER REALLY CHANGE?

Do people ever really change? That is a difficult question to answer and I have spent decades trying to figure this out. My theory has been pretty much consistent and I do not figure it will change too much at this point of my life. I believe for the most part, the **core** being of a person does not change. If you are a kind-hearted, considerate person, then those core characteristics will tend to stick with you, no matter how many horrible things have happened to you. I have tried to change that about myself and I never could. I felt that I was too nice and was always being taken advantage of. I would decide many times to try and not care as much, or not be so nice. I thought "nice guys/girls finish last" so I may as well change. But I couldn't...because that is not who I am. If you are the same type, then you have the best chance at evolving and growing. You care about others and you want to be the best person possible. You have healthy core values and qualities which will not change, but you are open to working on self-improvement. You can become stronger and make healthier decisions.

As much as it is difficult to change the core being of a person with endearing qualities, the same is true for those who have instilled negative traits. The people who lie, cheat, get easily angered or treat you poorly are less likely to change. They seem to be stuck in their selfish ways, and nothing matters beyond themselves. For most of my years, I would make excuses and justify people's bad behavior. I would always try and stay positive. I would see some glimmer of hope or goodness in them, and that would be enough for me to believe in their possibility to change. Then I realized, I have been through many more horrible things than them, and I do not treat people poorly. I did not understand those qualities that came out of a person because I did not possess them myself. I have learned many times, that if a person shows me those negative true colors, then it is in them and can come out at any time. That would scare me and I did not want to be in a position where I would be there when it did.

A PROBLEM NEEDS TO BE ACKNOWLEDGED

People do not have a chance at changing unless they are aware and acknowledge the problem. If you are expecting someone to change, who feels there is no problem, you will be wasting much valuable time.

PEOPLE DO NOT CHANGE UNLESS THEY WANT TO

They need to want to change. If someone changes for someone else, they almost always tend to go back to their old behavior. Not only that…they will tend to resent and blame the person whom they changed for. Some people are happy with the way they are.

NOTE TO SELF: EMPOWERMENT

SOMETHING DRASTIC HAS TO HAPPEN

A life-altering event has the power to change people...for the good or for the bad. People tend to change when they hit rock bottom, after a death, or a divorce etc. If something has caused a person a lot of pain or pushed them to their limit, there is a great possibility for change.

FACING DEATH

When someone is reaching the end of their life, they may spend a lot of time reflecting. They may have revelations or regret past behavior. I have recently experienced this. My entire life, a certain person had treated me poorly and close to the end of his life, there was a turnaround. I never, ever thought I would see this transformation, but I am extremely blessed to have been open to this possibility.

 Everybody has the ability to change, but it all comes down to if they want to or not. In the meantime, do not waste your time waiting around, especially if someone has a negative impact on your life and is stressing you out. If people are treating you poorly, then look at their actions, instead of their words. Stop listening to their apologies, excuses, and victimizing stories and look at their behavior...as it will not lie. If they are meant to change, they will...in their own time.

 Do people make you feel like you are a horrible person? You live your life the best way you can. You have a heart of gold and you are out for everyone's best interests. You would not hurt anyone, yet you never seem good enough. You feel like you are constantly walking on eggshells. It does not seem to make any sense. How are you such a horrible person? The truth is, not everyone is going to understand you and not everyone is going to like you. This may be tough to swallow.

Do not allow people to use fear, manipulation, or guilt over you. As soon as this happens, that is your signal to get away. Block them out mentally or physically remove yourself from them. You do not need to listen to this. No one should be talking to you like this, especially those people who are supposed to care about you and love you. You have a responsibility to protect your power within and not allow bullies to try and overpower you.

You may have listened to people who put you down. Maybe these are the wrong people to be listening to? If these destructive words are coming from family members, you may believe them to be true. I mean, they are biologically programmed to love you, aren't they? You may assume that they would not hurt you. Very often, the ones closest to you could be hurting you the most. Their words can become deep-rooted and you may have become conditioned to believe them. You may start to get down on yourself and start to believe that you *are* this horrible person. It is important to remember what is true and who you truly are. Did you forget how amazing you are and need to be reminded?

THEY ARE UNHAPPY

The people putting you down or not appreciating you, are on a lower vibration than you are. You may represent what they wish they could be, and you pose a threat to them. You know the saying "misery loves company"? If you do not lower yourself to their level, they cannot affect you.

DO NOT APOLOGIZE FOR BEING YOU

Are you making excuses or justifying yourself? It is important that you do not lose yourself, as there is only one you. Accept who you are and embrace yourself. You were brought into this world for a purpose. Do not allow anyone to destroy you and make you feel like you are a horrible person.

THE TRUTH ALWAYS COMES OUT

If people do not understand you now, they may later. We all have our own lessons and rate of growing. They may eventually catch up to you in time. In the meantime, focus your energy on more productive things. They may never reach the point of recognizing or acknowledging the truth. All you can be, is true to yourself. The right people will cherish you.

FIND YOUR TRIBE

We all have a group of people who we instantly connect with. These people understand that you are not a horrible person, without having to say a word. You do not have to defend yourself to these people, and you do not have to explain yourself. It is as though you have lived parallel lives and they *know* you. They have similar morals and beliefs. You can be yourself and you do not have to be afraid of being judged. These people love and support you more than many of your own family members do. Your tribe is out there. Be on a mission to find them. Your life will be easier and happier with them by your side.

Keep spreading the love and keep shining brightly. Compassionate, loving and positive people will flock towards you. These are the people who matter. These are the people who will lift you up, instead of knocking you down.

NOTE TO SELF: EXERCISES

1. Write on a piece of paper who are your safe people and who are the toxic ones in your life. Make 3 separate columns with the middle one listing the ones you are unsure of.
2. List your boundaries. What will you tolerate in a person? What will you not tolerate? Make your list, so your boundaries become crystal clear.

In the end, it does not matter if it is a parent, sibling, best friend, co-worker, or stranger. *No one deserves to be taken for granted or mistreated.* Do not tolerate or enable this behavior. Also, do not take it personally. Often those people are treating others the exact same way. You deserve and are worth more.

Take some time today to take care of yourself. Re-evaluate the people in your life. How do they make you feel? Do you feel better or worse after seeing or talking to them? Let your feelings be your guide. Get rid of the ones who are negatively impacting your life. They are slowly and continually corroding your soul, self-esteem and self-worth. Make space and time for the loving and supportive people. You're worth it!

6

STEP 4: SAY NO

My girls and I became my top priority. Anyone who was trying to destroy our bond or our lives, were immediately eliminated. We needed to heal and we needed to get stronger together. It was just the three of us. That was my entire life. Until I got our lives straightened, I did not take on anything else. We could not afford one more ounce of negativity in our lives.

When patients are in the Intensive Care Unit, they are immediately put into isolation. Anyone posing a threat to the critical patient's health, would be banned from seeing them. Their health and well-being are at the upmost importance because they are facing a life or death situation. Each moment is crucial.

I felt like a patient who was in the ICU. I have put myself last for way too long, that my life was in jeopardy. I had a consistently high resting heart rate of 111 beats per minute. When I checked my blood pressure at the local drugstore, the pharmacist could not believe how low my blood pressure was. He made me check it three times to make sure the extremely low numbers were correct, before he ordered me to immediately go the Emergency Room. The chronic stress would be difficult to come back from. My entire life was turned upside down. I had to take extreme measures in order to get myself "out of the woods". I at least had to get myself to a "stable condition". I could not risk going back to my old way of living.

I needed to conserve my energy. I could not waste it on any more nonsense. I could not even afford to attend gatherings and family functions. People who were used to having me at their disposal were not happy with this change. For the first time in my life, I started saying *no* to things. Many people and family members were mad at me, but I figured if they truly cared for me and my girls' well-being, then they would understand.

I reached a point, where it did not matter if anyone understood or not. This was something I needed to do. I did the work to figure out what my boundaries were. I knew what and who I was willing to tolerate in my life. I stayed true to this. I was at a pivotal point in my life and I had reached a crossroad. If we were going to survive this, I needed to take care of myself. I was the only person who I could really count on. My girls and their futures were depending on me, so they took precedence over everything. It was my girls who gave me the drive to turn everything around and I was not going to give up on them.

NOTE TO SELF: EMPOWERMENT

No matter how hard the challenges were ahead, I was going to face them with honesty and integrity. There were options presented to me which would involve having to cheat people out of money. Desperate times call for desperate measures, but that was not how I lived my life. I was not going that route. I finally knew who I truly was. God has shown me the light of truth during my darkest times. I was no longer deceived and I now have the gift of discernment. I could not be tempted by darkness. I have no fear, only love. I had extremely strong values and morals. I was not going to compromise or jeopardize myself for anything or anyone. As long as I stayed true to myself, I was willing to suffer any consequences and take full responsibility. It was much better than choosing to live my life as a lie. I did not want to regret making any decisions and I refused to go against the values of my core being. This was definitely not the easy way out, but I have complete trust in my divine guidance. With God, all things are possible.

I was starting to find my voice. I found that people were much happier when I stayed quiet and did not speak up against their wrongdoings. I had stayed quiet for so long, that they never expected that the truth would ever come out. They could no longer hide behind their lies. They could no longer turn the blame on me without me defending myself. I did not back down either. I endured a lot of criticism from family members when I had to boycott many family holidays and events. I was determined to stay true to myself. I noticed myself growing stronger and happier.

My girls and I were not going to risk having someone destroy all the progress we had made. My intuition and inner guidance grew as I started to believe in myself more and more. The work you've done in the last couple of steps will help your inner voice get louder also. Now that you no longer have the negative external distractions, you can start to believe in yourself again.

My path became clear and I knew exactly what I needed to do in order to continue moving forward. I had decided that it would be best to get a serving job for fast and easy money. I figured I would go back to the same restaurant I worked at in high school, since throughout the years, the managers were always asking me to come back. I also could not afford the extra pressure on me having to learn a new job. At this point, I was still fragile and could not handle additional stress. I thought it was perfect, because this Swiss Chalet was out of town and I would not have to face people I knew. I was tired of fake people pretending to care about me, when they only wanted the latest gossip. Also with a serving, I would not have to worry about taking my work home with me. This job was a means to an end, and I had the bigger picture in mind. I loved how I had money in my pocket every night, instead of having to wait every two weeks for my paycheck. Things were slowly looking up. We had a safe place to stay at my sister's house and we all meshed well as a family. It was nice to get closer to my sister, brother-in-law, niece and nephew. Each day was getting better.

If your present moment is not the greatest, trust and believe that things are only going to get better. What is happening right now is only the residual effect of your past choices. We are in the process of changing things for the better, and we are not going to look back. If you want to change your future, then we need to be making better choices today.

Learning to say *no* is not easy when you are a people pleaser. When people are used to you taking on that role, they have a difficult time when you start to say *no*. *What do you mean? You always say yes? You are always there.* The first thing that they will say is that you are selfish. When you hear someone call you that, *it is a red flag*. They are the selfish ones. They are not caring for your well-being and are trying to manipulate you. People who truly care about you will understand. You are not saying *no* to be mean, or to hurt somebody. You are saying *no* because you cannot or do not want to do something. That is your right. You do not need to apologize or explain yourself. You are understanding when people say *no* to you, so there is nothing wrong with expecting the same in return. A healthy relationship does not work when it is one-sided all the time.

There is a healthy balance when trying to please others. You can still be the giving and loving person that you are, but you also need to be giving and loving to yourself. Make sure that you allow yourself to receive, and are not the one continuing to self-sacrifice. Be conscious and protective of your kind heart.

CALLING ALL PEOPLE PLEASERS!

Pleasing everyone is impossible. It is natural to want to make the ones you love happy, but what about those of you who take people pleasing to a whole other level? You spend every day giving and doing things for others. You may even feel like you need to give more, and like it is never enough. You avoid conflict and confrontation at all costs. You say *yes*, when you really want to say *no*, and you put others' needs ahead of your own. Does this sound like you? If it does, I commend you for all of your selfless acts. It is sad if people are not appreciating or noticing all of your kind efforts. You truly have a great heart.

You would think that this extreme people pleasing behavior would make you feel wonderful. I mean, you surpass everyone around in thoughtfulness. A simple *thank you* would keep you satisfied and keep you going. You do not expect much in return, if anything at all. Yet often you feel taken advantage of, unappreciated, depleted, and maybe even lonely.

I can relate to all of you "people pleasers" and I have a huge soft spot for you. The world needs more loving, caring and thoughtful people such as yourself, but it is also important to find balance. I feel compelled to protect and preserve your kind heart. You deserve to feel the same amount of joy as what you are trying to impress upon everyone you meet.

PEOPLE PLEASING CAN CAUSE RESENTMENT

If you are wanting to say *no*, but you continue to say *yes*, you will build up resentment towards that person or situation. A simple "no" will rectify that problem.

DO NOT BE AFRAID TO SPEAK UP

You may be afraid to speak up because you may not want to disappoint someone or cause conflict. Pleasing others may be easier than "rocking the boat". Often times when you express what you want, you may be surprised to find out that others want the same thing, but may have also been too afraid to say so.

TAKE YOUR TIME WITH MAKING DECISIONS

If you try and please everyone, you may overcommit. If you do not want to attend a gathering, do not be afraid to say *no*. If you often find yourself in situations where you want to help and please everyone, tell them that you will think about it and get back to them. This is one of the most important tools that I have learned. It allows you the time to think about what you really want to do.

OUTER VALIDATION

If you are constantly searching for outer validation, you may become repeatedly disappointed. Your kind gestures and good deeds may not receive the warranted appreciation. If you are giving or trying to please others, and expecting them to validate you, then you will never be satisfied. Do what you feel is right in your heart and only if you are willing to do things without expectations.

"Do what you feel in your heart to be right, for you'll be criticized anyway."

-Eleanor Roosevelt

"No" was one of the first few words we learned. We had absolutely no trouble saying it as a young child. We used that word all the time. It made us feel strong, powerful and independent. We would repeatedly chant, "N.O. spells *NO!*" We would say it with such confidence and entitlement. There was never any explanation. If we needed to expand, we would simply repeat the word *no*, again and again. There was something automatic and easy about saying it.

Throughout life, things shifted. We began to learn that the word *no* was bad and what was tolerated as a toddler, was no longer "cute". Our parents told us not to disobey them or talk back. We would get reprimanded for using the word or standing up for ourselves. You learned that it often disappointed people. You quickly discovered that people were much happier when you said *yes*, so your *No, No, No*'s became a thing of the past. The word *no* got replaced with an *easier* and more *pleasing* word, which resulted in less conflict. You may have been unaware of this transformation because it may have been a slow and subtle evolution. Somehow, you became more focused on pleasing others, that your own happiness may have been disregarded or sacrificed in the process.

YOU CAN CHANGE THE RULES AND SAY NO

If certain people are taking advantage of your good nature, do not be afraid to change the rules. You can say *no*. You may have made commitments and promises, but if someone is taking you for granted, you have a choice to no longer allow this type of treatment or expectations.

TAKE YOUR TIME

There is no rush for an answer. If someone is pushing you, simply say, "I will get back to you" and give yourself time to think about it. *Do not feel pressured into committing to something that you may regret or not be able to follow through with later.*

STAY TRUE TO YOURSELF

If something does not feel right, say *no*. If it goes against your core beliefs and values, do not compromise who you are.

LOOK AFTER YOURSELF

You can have all the good intentions in the world, but you need to take care of yourself. You may feel drained, require sleep or need to take it easy. It may be difficult if you have already committed to something or have people counting on you. But if things have changed and you are no longer in a position to attend or help, you need to say *no*. Do not feel bad, because people who care about you will understand. If they don't, it is best that you figure this out sooner than later. You will not be of any good to yourself or anyone else, if you do not take care of yourself first.

    Self-care is vitally important. Many of us were brought up believing that if we put ourselves first, that we are being selfish. As a result, we sacrifice our own happiness. We push ourselves beyond our limits to the point of depletion. We work so hard and forget to use the word *no*.

We choose to ignore the fact that we should slow down and we do not stop until we get sick or become utterly exhausted.

If you are thinking that it is selfish to take time for yourself, I am here to tell you otherwise. I have learned this lesson many times over. Even though I try to balance my life the best I can, I still need to be reminded every now and again.

IT IS NOT SELFISH TO TAKE CARE OF YOUR HEALTH

Your health is the most important. Remember to not take it for granted.

BURNING THE CANDLE AT BOTH ENDS

If you are trying to do too much at once, you will eventually get burnt out. It can take weeks or even months to fully recharge. If you take a few moments a day to slow down and meditate, you will be amazed at the difference it can make in your life. You especially need to do this during times when you feel overwhelmed and have no time for yourself. Slow and steady wins the race.

LISTEN TO YOUR BODY

Your body will let you know when you need to take a break.

PUT YOUR OXYGEN MASK ON FIRST

The flight attendant always tells you to put your own oxygen mask on first before you try and assist others. This is not being selfish. This is so you are at your best, with full strength to be there for others.

You cannot please or save everyone. Of course you want to be able to do all the fun things that you are invited to, or help all of the people that need your help. It can become overwhelming and extremely draining, especially if you are pleasing the wrong people. This can leave you with no time or energy for the ones who hold top priority in your life, and quite often put the fewest demands on you. There will be people who may not be happy when you start saying *no*. It can be difficult when you have been spending your life trying to avoid conflict. You are just one person and there is only so much of you that can go around. Make saying *no*, as simple as it once was when you were a child. *It frees up more time for you to say yes to things that make you happiest and are the most important.*

Do you have friends or even strangers treating you better than your own family? This has to make you think. Ideally in a perfect world, it would be amazing if you could count on your family for love and support. There are families out there like this. If you are less fortunate, at some point, you do need to decide on your boundaries. It is not worth having such a negative impact on your life. You have a choice to not allow this destructive treatment towards you.

I have had to walk away from a few family members in order to self-protect. I chose to no longer have people treat me poorly. Family or no family, it is not right! I got tired of justifying their bad behavior and trying to make sense of it. Also, if it is not working, stop forcing it.

Sometimes the best thing is to let it go, forgive and send love.

Hopefully, in the future there can be a reconnection in a better space. You may need to accept that they are not on the same level as you. They need to work on themselves, in their own time and do their own inner work. You need to decide what you are able to handle and what you are willing to tolerate.

Focus on people who build you up higher every day. Family can be blood-related, but they can also be friends and other kind people. They are the ones who make you feel good and are there for you. They are the people who unconditionally love you and the ones who matter most in your life. They are looking out for your well-being and have your best interests at heart. This is your family. Decide what family is to you and create your unconditionally loving and supportive family - whether or not they are blood-related.

STAY SILENT

Remember those people you figured out were toxic in your life? Hopefully, you found the strength to separate yourself from them. It is important to stay firm and not back down from your decision. It is best to stay silent and not waste your breath.

ARE YOU SELF-SABOTAGING AN AMAZING LIFE?

Self-sabotaging is a very common behavior. Just when things are about to get good, do you wreck it for yourself? I have done this numerous times. It all boils down to low self-esteem and low self-worth. You believe it is too good to be true. Even though you want these good things or amazing people in your life, somehow you are not able to accept this for yourself. It may seem foreign to you. You may not know how to handle a great relationship or things going well, because it may be unfamiliar to you. Although you know it is wrong, you feel more familiar and comfortable with tumultuous relationships and drama. Are you your own worst enemy? Are you wanting to improve your life, but make choices that would show the opposite?

I recently bumped into someone who was so excited about improving her self-worth. I looked at her and I could not help but share in her excitement. She was on the right path. She seemed stronger and happier, but then she proceeded to tell me that she got back together with her ex-boyfriend. She was so close to improving that area of her life, then she self-sabotaged it and regressed.

I cannot even tell you how many times the two of them have broken up and gotten back together. Clearly, their relationship is not meant to be. People who often self-sabotage, tend to make excuses and justify bad behavior. She said that she was learning lessons. You cannot argue with that, but hasn't she already learned these lessons by now? From the outside looking in...the message seems clear. I guess when it comes to the matters of the heart, somehow your heart distorts these valuable lessons.

IT DOES NOT HAVE TO BE SO DIFFICULT

You only get back together because time has passed, you got stronger and you are only remembering the good things. Now knowing better, I have learned that life does not need to be so difficult and a struggle. I only thought that was how it was supposed to be, because that was all I had ever known. I could never imagine that life and love could be so easy. You should not have to *force* your relationships, friendships or any area in your life to work. When you are following your natural rhythm and flow of the Universe, your life will be full of ease, happiness and abundance.

DO NOT GIVE UP

If you are trying to break a bad habit or pattern, it can be difficult at first. This is when you are at your greatest risk of self-sabotaging. You may fail at first and become discouraged, but it is important to not give up. Be kind to yourself. This has been your only way of life, and now you are changing your way of thinking, behaving and natural tendencies. It will get easier, as you get used to your new and improved way of life.

LET'S TALK ABOUT RELATIONSHIPS

How are your relationships and friendships? Do you feel fulfilled with your partner? Or are you feeling like something is missing and you are losing yourself in the process? Things were great in the beginning, then all of a sudden you find yourself in another crappy relationship. You cannot believe it happened *again*! You were not going to allow yourself to be treated poorly, lied to or taken advantage of. You feel hurt, betrayed, drained and possibly numb.

NOTE TO SELF: EMPOWERMENT

Some of you are alone because you are unable to find someone. You feel ready, but you cannot seem to find the right one. Maybe you are alone because you have been hurt too badly? Being by yourself may seem better than dealing with the aggravation which relationships tend to bring.

It is ironic that I am talking about relationships. My relationships were nothing short of tumultuous. Not only my romantic relationships, but also my relationships with some family members and friends. Somehow, all of the amazing people in my life were being overshadowed by all of the toxic people. The selfish, abusive, and manipulative people crept their way into the forefront of my life.

When it came to romantic relationships, I seriously thought I would *never* get that area of my life right. I accepted that as my fate. I have grown up never witnessing a healthy or loving relationship. My mother passed away, never getting a relationship right. I felt I was doomed for failure in relationships as well. I did not make the greatest choices. I pushed away the nice guys because I found them boring or too good to be true. I would not allow myself to get attached, as I could not handle my heart being ripped out.

Do not give up on relationships. I have been where you are at. I will help you find the unconditional love you deserve.

DO NOT LOSE YOURSELF

Do not compromise your beliefs, morals and what you stand for. Do not lose yourself in a relationship. You do not want it ending with you having to put yourself back together. You build them up and they end up better, yet you are left feeling used, abused, and drained. You should not have to fight for their attention and constantly try to please them.

ENHANCE EACH OTHER'S LIVES

Healthy relationships allow each other to grow, learn, play, and laugh together. You should both be fine alone, but together you enhance each other's lives. You are free to be yourself and are loved unconditionally.

YOUR RELATIONSHIPS ARE ALL DIFFERENT

Each relationship is different, so give this new person a chance. Do not let a bad experience from the past carry over and wreck something good. Do not shut your heart down because you have been hurt or betrayed.

BE PATIENT

There is no rush. You do not want to settle. If you have been hurt in the past, it is wise to proceed with caution. It is only a matter of time before people will show you their true colors. You deserve to be treated well in all relationships. It will be worth the wait.

The relationships in your life are the cause of the majority of the stress and happiness in your life. Choose each relationship and friendship wisely.

NOTE TO SELF: EXERCISES

Write down the list of your ideal mate. Write down the qualities which you require in a compatible relationship. This allows you to think with your head first. What works for you? What are the deal breakers? Very often, once we are in a relationship, our judgement can become clouded. It is extremely helpful to be aware of this before you enter a relationship, when your head is clear. Keep true to what you require and desire, and you will be well on your way to a healthy relationship.

Who do you need to start saying *no* to?

1.

2.

3.

List 3 of your priorities:

1.

2.

3.

List 3 things you can eliminate out of your life and would lift an incredible weight off of you:

1.

2

3.

List 3 things you can use some help with:

1.

2.

3.

When you say no, you make more room for those who matter most.

7

STEP 5: THINK POSITIVE AND SHOW GRATITUDE

I kept my promise to my sister Lisa and was out of her house within the 4 months. I could not believe that was possible, since there was a lot of picking up and cleaning up to do in my life. I was able to save up for first and last month's rent. I found an apartment that was central to both of my daughters' schools. It was not the best apartment, but I was able to get it on my own with my blemished credit and new job. It allowed me to keep my word and my girls and I now had our *own* place. In four months, I went from losing my house, my possessions, money, dignity and pride, to getting back on my feet. I believed I could do it, even while others doubted me.

Before I lost everything, I had it all. I had a nice house, a great full-time job, a new SUV, a lifestyle of concerts and sporting events, and was rubbing shoulders with celebrities. I was a trendsetter wearing my hair and clothes years ahead of the latest fashions. The only thing lacking in my life was a loving, healthy relationship. I was attracting people who were liking me for what I had and for what I looked like. I was not finding people who truly liked me for the amazing person I was on the inside. It was only when it was too late, that they realize this. In my head I could picture what it would be like to have an amazing man and a great relationship, but that was only in my imagination. When I came back to my reality, these types of men and relationships did not exist in the forefront of my life.

Deep down inside, I wanted a relationship. I knew that I would not settle. I would rather stay alone forever, than deal with the stress of another wrong partner. People assumed I had trouble with settling down. I would always say, *"I have no problem with settling down, I have a problem with settling."* I had made a vision board back in 2008. I placed it on top of my dresser by the foot of my bed. That way it would be the first thing I saw in the morning and the last thing I saw at night. I would also stare at it during the day, while I was writing in bed.

I made my vision board out of a large thick piece of paper, similar to Bristol board. I first heard about a vision board while watching the documentary, *The Secret*. The film primarily talked about the law of attraction. It was a great reminder of how you bring about what you think about. The philosophy is that *like attracts like*. If you are focusing on negative things or thoughts, more negative things and thoughts will come. You clearly want to focus on positive thinking to turn your life into a positive direction.

NOTE TO SELF: EMPOWERMENT

When you make a vision board, dream big. Put pictures of anything you desire in life, inspirational words, and also things that make you feel good. The purpose of the vision board is to stay focused and positive. When you look at all the pictures on it which you desire, believe in your heart that they are coming. Focus heavily on feeling as though you already have those things.

With me, I divided my vision board into three sections. The more specific the better. That way it seems more real. On the left, I put a picture of a tall, dark handsome man, cuddling with a beautiful blonde lady. This was to demonstrate the sort of man that I wanted in my life. Visualize everything about this person, so when you meet him, you will know. I thought of the qualities in a man which I desired, and also the ones I knew would be compatible with me. I figured I would do this while I was clear-headed. Once you are in a relationship, your heart starts to get involved and your judgement may start to get clouded. This way I knew what I wanted beforehand and I would not settle for what fell into my lap.

It is sort of like when you go to a car dealership. You know you want a car, but really have not put too much thought into it. The car salesman can sweet talk you into buying some used car that you end up being completely dissatisfied with. But imagine if you know *exactly* what you want. You know the color, the year, the make, the model, all the accessories you desire, the price range etc. Then there is absolutely no way that anyone could sway you away from what you want. You know precisely what you are looking for. You know what will make you happy and you will not settle for anything less. This is how focused you can be with your life. You can have anything you desire, if you know what you want and believe you can get it. Obviously, the key is to take the necessary actions towards this. You cannot keep wishing for things and not take any action.

Every single person I know who made a list of what they desired in a partner, has had that person come into their life within a year - myself included. This is my exact list of compatible qualities and desires which I had on my vision board:

1. Honesty (So honest that people actually have trouble with it & don't know how to handle it)
2. Loyal
3. Outgoing
4. Makes me laugh
5. Good/Fun in bed
6. Likes to go out and watch sporting events (mainly hockey)
7. Loves music – loves to go to concerts or pubs with live music
8. Loves to dance & have fun
9. Not afraid to be themselves around me
10. He lets me be myself and loves me for it
11. Not jealous
12. Secure with himself
13. Secure with me
14. NO addictions of any sort
15. Believes in himself
16. Believes in me
17. Stands up for himself
18. Stands up for me
19. Easygoing
20. Tall

21. Dark hair/eyes
22. Handsome
23. Has an Edge
24. Reliable
25. Respects me
26. Thinks the world of me
27. Treats my children as if they were his own
28. Raises his children as I would...no children then agrees with my parenting skills
29. Understands me
30. Creative
31. Makes me feel secure and comfortable

That was my list. At this point, I knew which things were important to me. I understood myself enough to know what I needed in a healthy relationship, and what the deal breakers were. With this list, it held me accountable and true to what was best for me. If I met someone and they lied to me, I would check my list and see that honesty was number one. I have been lied to in the past way too many times, that I only wanted the truth. I was not going to tolerate any sort of lie right away, as I knew ultimately the relationship would be doomed. This saved me a lot of wasted time and heartache. I already had enough of that, and was determined to change this.

What works for you, may be completely different. What you want, and what you don't want should be clear to you at this point. We have done quite a bit of inner work over the last four steps, to be able to figure it out. Be as honest and specific as possible.

Everyone is different. It was important for a girlfriend of mine to have a man who gets his hair done in a hair salon, instead of a barber. For whatever reason that was extremely important to her. She ended up finding exactly that man! I cannot stress enough, the importance of getting clear with your goals and desires.

    I will share a bit more of what was on my board to spark some ideas of what to put on your own, if you decide to make one. Keep in mind that this was at the beginning of me finding out about a vision board, so I did not fully believe it would work at the time of making it. I was so desperate for my life to be better, that I thought it would be worth a try. Also, we only had a limited amount of magazines at the time, so there were not many options for cutouts. Some of the words or phrases I used were ones that caught my eye. Because I love to write, I had a lot of inspirational words to keep me in a positive mindset. You can put on your favorite quotes also or add pictures that inspire you. I put words like:

    Dream big, health, capture the moment, think positive, bring it, happiness, TRUTH, visualize, afford the best, balance, think you can, the choice is yours, true love, Los Angeles, RESPECT, peace, love.

I also wrote out:

1. ASK
2. BELIEVE
3. RECEIVE

"Whatever the mind of man can conceive, it can achieve."

-W. Element Stone 1902-2002

NOTE TO SELF: EMPOWERMENT

"Follow your bliss and the Universe will open doors for you where there were only walls."

-Joseph Campbell 1904-1987

In the center of my board I drew a picture of my envisioned book with the title *#1 National Best Seller* on top. The remainder of the space was filled up with pictures and some important items to me. I glued on my orange ticket which I received when I went to L.A. to attend *The Price is Right* Show. This had always been a dream of mine. I had watched *The Price is Right* and *The Young and the Restless* every summer at my grandparent's house growing up as a child. These were my grandmother's favorite shows. I was extremely close to my grandmother, and my sisters and I would watch along with her.

    I made it to Los Angeles for the taping of the show. I was excited as the original host, Bob Barker was going to retire and I made it before he did. I found it strange that when we approached the gate at CBS Studios, there was no lineup. On the gate, there was a sign apologizing that the shows were canceled for the entire week that I would be there. Bob Barker had hurt his foot and was unable to host the show. It was a disappointment, so that is why I put it on my board. I was determined to go back and attend the show again. I also put on some pictures of Europe. A couple of times during my childhood, my father got my sisters and I all excited by telling us he was going to take us, only to find out that they were empty promises. I decided to take it upon myself to travel to Europe. I did not know how I was going to get there, but I believed I would. Here is another important point. The "how" is not important. You do not have to worry about *how* things will come about. You just need to believe that they *will*, and trust the Universe to shift and align to make it happen for you.

I put pictures of beaches and a picture of a couple getting a massage on the beach. (I always thought that would be relaxing). I had a fake $1,000,000 bill and glued that on also. Why not? I had a bunch of guitars all over the top right corner, as I love music and guitars. The top center has a plane and I wrote "Mile High Club" on it (don't judge). I also put a picture of Ellen DeGeneres and Oprah, as I could see myself one day being on their show, after my book was published.

I had also received a little card that had the Peace Prayer of St. Francis of Assisi. This was my mother's favorite prayer and has resonated with me my entire life:

Lord, make me an instrument of your peace.
Where there is hatred, let me sow love;
Where there is injury, pardon;
Where there is doubt, faith;
Where there is despair, hope;
Where there is darkness, light;
O Divine Master, grant that I may not so much seek
To be consoled, as to console;
To be understood, as to understand;
To be loved, as to love.
For it is in giving that we receive;
It is in pardoning that we are pardoned;
And it is in dying that we are born to eternal life.
Amen.

This vision board is what helped me to keep thinking positively. It also helped me to focus on a bright future, instead of dwelling on the past.

MANIFESTING

Positive thinking and positive action will change your life. If you have endured many years of listening to others put you down, discourage you or be negative, then you would naturally be conditioned to have negative thoughts about yourself. It becomes automatic. You become your own worst critic and extremely hard on yourself. It is important that you consciously undo this negative conditioning. It is not going to be easy to retrain your brain, but it is imperative that you immediately replace all negative thoughts with positive ones. *Positive thinking is the only avenue to true success, peace and happiness.*

Now that you removed or limited the negative people, you do not have to listen to them putting you down or making you feel guilty. The majority of the drama in your life will be eliminated by this one single step. You will quiet down the voices in your head that are self-destructive.

POSITIVE THINKING AND THE ELASTIC BAND

Some people wear an elastic band to help bring awareness to any bad habit they are trying to break. You can also use this technique, if you want to stop negative thinking and switch to positive thinking. Simply wear an elastic band around your wrist (not too tight to cut off circulation, but tight enough to feel a little snap on your wrist when pulled). Each time you catch yourself having any sort of negative thoughts, snap the elastic band. You want to stop the negativity immediately, so you do not build up negative momentum. You want to prevent turning your day/life into a downward spiral. Shift your negative thoughts and focus on something positive. This is a great tool to help bring awareness to each moment and action. It can help undo a negative pattern which has become completely automatic.

AFFIRMATIONS

Using positive affirmations are an excellent way to take control of negative self-talk. They are positive phrases that you repeat over and over again to change a negative belief. If someone has repeatedly told you that you are fat, ugly, stupid or will never be good enough, then you have many years of undoing. Affirmations are a great way to change these negative beliefs and will positively change your life. Louise Hay is a great advocate for using affirmations. You can receive a daily affirmation from her website.

MOTIVATIONAL BOOKS AND VIDEOS

Reading inspirational books and videos will help you to think positively. There are many out there. Dr. Wayne Dyer is known as the "Father of Motivation" and he has written over 40 books, which have positively helped to change many lives.

If you are tired of being your own worst critic, then positive thinking is the way to go. It will help you to be more productive and also help end any pain or suffering. You will be more pleasurable to be around, especially for positive people. You will believe in yourself and become more confident in your own power. Your positive mindset will help you to achieve great things, which will lead you to a joyous and fulfilling life.

YOU ARE WORTH AS MUCH AS OPRAH

Self-worth is the determining factor of your total worth. It influences how rich your relationships are, the extent of your happiness, the amount of your income...and in fact your entire life. Everyone knows that Oprah makes a ton of money. But deeper than that, she has a strong sense of self-worth and values. She is not afraid to walk away in order to hold out for what she feels she deserves and what is right. She stays true to herself. Her high self-worth, persistence, hard work and strong core values are what helped her get to where she is today. You have the exact same power within you to be worth as much as Oprah.

Many times people devalue themselves because they have low self-worth and a shattered self-esteem. This is caused by growing up with someone close to you repeatedly putting you down. You start to feel like you can never be good enough. Also, if you made some big mistakes in the past, you may feel guilt and regret, which may also diminish your value. The majority of people have gone through many struggles and have had someone important to them repeatedly put them down. It is important to realize that regardless of what was said or done in the past, *you are worth more.*

RAISE YOUR SELF-WORTH

It is important to know your value. You have your own unique personality, strengths and talents that only *you* can offer this world. Awareness of this brings about a greater confidence and raises your self-worth. You will not tolerate people making you feel less worthy. Your life will just go up from here.

LET GO OF THE PAST

We are all human and have all made mistakes or bad choices. We are continually learning and growing. You have the power in this very moment to decide to turn things around. Whatever negative things you or someone else has said or done prior to this moment, will no longer negatively affect you.

DO NOT SELL YOURSELF SHORT

Hold out for what you want and what you feel you deserve. If in your heart, you feel something is not right or serving you well, stick to what you feel is. It is amazing how the right people and the right situations will rise up to your level.

DO NOT WASTE YOUR TIME EXPLAINING YOURSELF

There is no need to continually try and prove or explain your worth to someone who clearly does not appreciate or recognize your magnificence. You should not be in a position where you feel you need to apologize to anyone for who you are. You are wasting your valuable time. Stay true to yourself and remember your worth.

I believe your inner and outer values interrelate. Ultimately, only you can determine your worth and how you will allow others to treat you. Once you work on the inside, your outer world will reflect this upgrade. We all have the same power as Oprah, or anyone else who you feel holds more value than yourself. Knowing that we are all born with this same power, is empowering in itself. Do not hold yourself back. When you truly understand the extent of your worth, you will have unlimited possibilities and prosperity.

It is extremely important to continue to rise above the negativity. As you continue to lift higher and higher, you will be introduced to people on that higher vibration. These people will exude positivity. They will value you, understand you, respect you and enhance your life.

YOUR NATURAL FLOW IS GUIDING YOU

There is a natural flow to your life. Pay attention to the doors that are continuing to open or close in your life. The Universe will shut doors to things which are not meant for your higher good. Other doors will continue to open, until you begin to understand that it is the best direction or choice for you. Bring a greater awareness to what is happening around you and what people are saying to you. Often this is where you may find many of the answers you are looking for and the path of least resistance.

"Everything happens for a reason. Sometimes good things fall apart, so better things can come together."

-Marilyn Monroe

ACCEPT THAT EVERYTHING HAPPENS FOR A REASON

There is a great relief and comfort that comes with trusting that everything happens for a reason - especially when you feel like you made a mistake, a bad choice or something horrible has happened. It helps to know that there is a higher purpose. There is a divine progression and order to the natural unfolding of your life. It can be challenging to find faith in this when you get caught up in the emotions of an event. The older and wiser you get, the more you may begin to realize that everything truly does happen for a reason.

When you look back at all the pieces of your life, it becomes clearer. In retrospect you may say, "Well, this wouldn't have happened, if this didn't happen" or "I wouldn't have met this person, if this didn't happen the way it did". But too often, we want answers right now. We want to make sense of it all and understand why things are happening. It can become frustrating if we cannot rationalize it.

We cannot control the outer circumstances. All we can do is the best we can with moving towards the direction we want to go. I am not saying that you should put your life on autopilot and not be conscious of your choices and decisions. It is important to live your life with purpose and intent. When you combine this with the natural flow, you will be more accepting and open to all life has to offer. Trust the journey.

YOUR INNER WORLD

Your inner world is all you really have control of. Your outside world can seem chaotic and crazy, but you have the choice to stay in control, positive and unaffected. Other people or things around you may affect your mood, your day, or even your entire life. The nature of how you feel may depend upon what happens. If people around you are positive and things are going right, then you have an amazing day. If you are surrounded by people who are complaining, putting you down, or are negative, then you have a horrible day. The lack of control of these exterior factors in your life, can become extremely challenging. You may feel like there is nothing you can do. We can try our hardest to be positive and kind, yet sometimes we may not receive the same back from others. If you control your inner world, your outer world will no longer affect or control you or your emotions. Not a single person or thing has the power to make you feel a certain way, except for you. How powerful is that?

MEDITATING

Meditation is one of the best ways to clear out all the clutter in your mind and your outside world. It connects you back to your true self. It is a great tool to relieve anxiety and stress. Meditation will bring you to a place of stillness, calmness, clarity and peace.

YOGA

Yoga will help you to control your inner world. It took me many years to calm down my inner and outer world enough to appreciate this amazing form of exercise. It is a great way to connect your body, mind and spirit.

BREATHE

When people are not being kind or you find yourself in a difficult situation, take a few deep breaths. This gives you time to access the situation, before you allow it to take over you.

WALK IN NATURE

Connecting to nature or walking along the beach also helps you to connect to your inner world.

RELEASE THROUGH EXPRESSION

Writing can help you release any exterior factors that are trying to control your inner world. Talking to a trusted friend is another way to let go of any negative emotions. Anxiety and stress are indicators that things need to change. Unfortunately, you cannot depend or wait for others to change their negative behavior. The only things you have the power to change, are your thoughts and your actions. It is important to get in touch and in control of your inner world, so your answers will be revealed to you. You will hopefully find that all the exterior factors will no longer matter, or affect you. *Once your inner voice and confidence have more power than anything else going on externally, you will have mastered your life.*

IT IS ALL ABOUT THE ATTITUDE OF GRATITUTE

When I focused on expressing gratitude, I really started to notice my internal shift. There is a lot of power in focusing on what you do have, instead of all the things you don't have and are going wrong. My incredible inner strength came back! Or did it ever leave? This step of showing gratitude is an important one also.

START YOUR DAY WITH GRATITUDE

Many people start off their day by giving thanks. You can express thanks for being alive. You can be grateful that it is a brand new day and you can begin the day with a "fresh" start. No matter how big or small, there is always something you can be grateful for. This will start your day off with a positive mindset.

KEEP A GRATITUDE JOURNAL

You can list 3-10 things in a journal that you are grateful for each day. This can become a wonderful daily habit. It can help you take a deeper look at what or who is making you the happiest. It can be helpful for those suffering from depression.

WRITE THANK YOU NOTES

It is nice to feel appreciated. Write a thank you note and give it to someone who you feel deserves recognition. If you do not want to give a thank you card, then an e-mail, text, or phone call will do just fine. This simple gesture can create such a positive impact to both you and the recipient.

RISE ABOVE THE NEGATIVITY

As you rise higher, you will become less tolerant of negativity. You become more sensitive and it begins to feel heavier than you remember. The weight of the energy becomes unbearable and you do not want anything to do with it. It is best to rise above it all.

    Recently, my two daughters and I have been subjected to an overwhelming amount of negativity. I found myself back into the familiar position of being the outcast and the black sheep because I did not fit in. I was extremely uncomfortable with what others seemed to enjoy and participated in. Except this time, I had my two daughters, by my side. The three of us are instilled with the same strong values and morals. We tried to rationalize and bring awareness to some truth, but it wouldn't be had. We tried to interrupt relentless negativity and switch it to positive energy, but our efforts were dismissed, unwelcomed and ignored. If we were to continue trying to defend and unveil the truth, it would have turned into a disaster. Negative people are set in their ways. You cannot reason with them or call them out on their wrongdoings. It is not worth the time and aggravation to deal with them. I have learned this lesson many times over.

"Never argue with stupid people, they will drag you down to their level and then beat you with experience."

-Mark Twain

KEEP SHINING

If you are not getting anywhere and the other person is not on the same vibration as you to comprehend what you are saying...walk away. Refuse to lower down to their level. Make a choice to continue to rise above and shine.

SEND OUT POSITIVITY AND LOVE

If you engage in the negativity, then it will add more fuel and momentum to it. Instead, be positive and show compassion. Sometimes that can be enough to turn things around.

SPEAK TRUTH

Defending yourself and others with the truth is all you can do. You cannot control how others will react. They may not recognize, accept, or understand what you are trying to say...until later. You did your due diligence and can now have peace with letting it go.

*****

Positive people surround themselves with positive people. Negative people do not connect well with happy people, and tend to stick to their own kind. Energy is contagious either way. You can decide which direction you want to go. If you chose positive thinking and positive people, you will have much less stress in your life.

NOTE TO SELF: EXERCISES

1. Make your list of qualities you desire in a partner that will be compatible with you.
2. Create a vision board to encourage positive thinking and goal setting. Do not worry about how it is all going to come about, just believe wholeheartedly that it will.
3. Write down what you are grateful for daily.

8

STEP 6: FORGIVE AND TAKE YOUR POWER BACK

Forgive? How can you forgive someone who has hurt you, betrayed you or has done something that you feel is unforgivable? That is exactly how I felt when my aunt suggested that I forgive my sister. I felt hurt by her for decades and she was not there for me when I needed her the most. I would try to forgive her and things would seem alright for a little while. Then after enough time had passed, the hurtful behavior would start again. It would be the same routine over and over again. I kept making excuses for Stacy, hoping things would change. I had decided that I was not going to put myself through this again. This time, I was *really* done. I remember thinking my aunt was crazy when she nonchalantly said, "Forgive her." I felt as though, she was disregarding everything I had expressed to her and that she truly did not understand the compiling pain that I was enduring. I was tired of being foolish and I was tired of being hurt. Not just by my sister, but by many people. Something had to change, and the furthest thing from my mind at the time was forgiveness.

    I had so many walls built up to protect me that it was impossible for anyone to get inside. After taking some time to heal and think clearly, I had decided to let down my walls and forgive once again. I could not believe I had reached that point. Even though I was tired of being hurt and angry, I never thought I could forgive certain people. But it seemed different this time.

    One of my best decisions in my life, was when I *truly* tried to forgive. I had decided that the past was no longer going to have a hold on me. I was not going to allow people to have any more power over me and my emotions. I cannot control what they do or how they treat me, but I can control whether or not I let it affect me. I needed to let it *all* go. Things had been weighing on me for way too long. I took on forgiveness with a new perspective, understanding and approach.

    Forgiveness is the key to taking your power back. Is there someone you are struggling to forgive? It is not about right or wrong - it is about letting go. I have completely forgiven my sister. I had distanced myself from her for years. My girls and I did not speak to her, and we did not attend family gatherings where she would be. This was our choice and our process. I felt bad for my sister Lisa who was stuck in the middle, but it was what we needed to do. I needed to get stronger so I would be better prepared for potentially harmful situations. I got so strong, that nobody could tear me down again. I now feel like I can be in any situation with anyone, and will be able to come out strong and unaffected.

I shared about my relationship with my sister for a reason. Many people struggle with family members and they become estranged. They hold on to the anger and no one gives in. They become stubborn and refuse to be the one who budges. If you have been hurt too many times, I can understand why you would not want to go back there.

I am hoping that my story with my sister inspires you. When you find your purpose, you will find that all fears transcends. Your passion pushes through any fear. That is why I have been open with sharing, because I know my stories help people. I am confident that my purpose is to pass along my wisdom in order to ease people's pain. I had to explain my story somewhat. I wanted you to understand a bit of the history, so you could get a sense of why I cut her out of my life for so many years, yet allowed her back in. That way, if you are in a similar situation with your sibling or family member, maybe our story can offer you hope of a reconciliation and healing.

Life is much better and freeing since I forgave my sister. We spent years blaming each other and avoiding accountability. We decided to agree to disagree and let bygones be bygones. The past no longer holds any power over me. The pain and anger vanished immediately. If I knew how good forgiveness would feel, I would have done it years ago. No one had ever told me. They would tell me to forgive, but they would never give me a good reason why.

FORGIVE BY ACCEPTING PEOPLE AS THEY ARE

When you accept people as they are, you will not be as disappointed. It is important to forgive the past and start new, if you want to move forward. The mistake people make is when they hope or believe that people will change. It is great if they do, but in the meantime you either need to accept them as they are, or let them go. Otherwise, you will continue to get hurt and frustrated.

FORGIVE AND SET BOUNDARIES

You have a choice to set boundaries of what you are willing or not willing to accept. This is the greatest tool you can use to self-protect and demonstrate self-love. There is nothing wrong with forgiving someone, but set a limit on the negative behavior.

FORGIVE AND BECOME EMPOWERED

You will gain inner strength and become empowered when you forgive. It feels great when you become aware that others do not have a hold or negative impact on your life, unless you allow them to. You have the power to forgive and be happy.

FORGIVE AND RELEASE PAIN/ANGER

When you forgive, you release all the past hurt and anger. You no longer allow those negative emotions to impact your present life. There is something magical and freeing about forgiveness. There will no longer be an anchor weighing you down. Take your power back. Forgive so you will feel lighter and happier.

FORGIVENESS IS THE KEY TO LETTING GO

Forgiveness does not mean that the behavior or actions of the hurtful person is acceptable. You are choosing to let go of the pain it caused you. This one helped me...*accept the apology you will never get!*

FORGIVE YOURSELF

You need to stop being so hard on yourself. Whatever has happened before this very moment cannot be changed. The words said cannot be taken back. All you can do is accept this, forgive others, forgive yourself, and make better choices moving forward.

10 PERFECT REASONS TO NOT BE A PERFECTIONIST

Perfectionists are too busy being "perfect". They need to be the best and excel at everything. When you are a perfectionist, you believe that there is only one right way; which is the "perfect" way. You spend your life trying to keep up to these unrealistic and often impossible to reach standards. You get disappointed because no one else can do things as perfectly as you can. You end up doing most of the things yourself.

If you are a people pleaser, then you are most likely a perfectionist. From experience, the two often go hand-in-hand. You may be too busy trying to please people and perfecting things that you may not have much time to think. You may have the belief that there is nothing better than being perfect right? It took me many years to figure out that life gets much better when you stop being a perfectionist.

1. A RECOVERED PERFECTIONIST CAN ACHIEVE EXCELLENCE MUCH FASTER

You already have the qualities and the drive to become a high-achiever. Without the impossible limitations, you are well ahead of the game.

2. MORE RELAXED

You become less uptight and can enjoy your natural, amazing life and the people around you. You will no longer freak out when things do not go completely as planned. You stop putting so much pressure and impossible demands on yourself and others.

3. LIVE LIFE TO THE FULLEST

You will live your life without the fear of making mistakes or being judged. You will be able to put yourself out there in the world and do the things you have always wanted to do.

4. MORE FUN

You will be less rigid, softer, and more accepting. You and others will have more fun.

5. MORE ENERGY

It is draining trying to be in control of everything all the time. Living a completely impossible lifestyle is hard to keep up to.

6. MORE OPEN-MINDED

Without the belief of only one right way, you will open your mind up to more possibilities. You will be open to accepting the natural flow and unexpected twists life throws in.

7. EASIER LIFE

As you let go of the fact that everything needs to be so "perfect", you will let competent people help you and make your life easier. Also you will let go of the things that really do not matter in the big picture.

8. MORE TIME

As you let go of impossible expectations and allow the help of competent people, you will have more time.

9. SENSE OF ACCOMPLISHMENT

Without the unrealistic demands and expectations, you will feel more accomplished. You will be able to succeed at being the best version of yourself.

10. BECOME HUMAN

Instead of continually being Superman or Wonder Woman, you become human. People will relate to you better because you become more resonating and authentic.

It is an amazing quality to want to strive towards excellence and be the best version of you. Push yourself beyond your limits. Do not let the perfectionist in you limit your dreams and prevent you from living a fulfilling life. You were born to be AWESOME!!!

STRENGTH

Whenever people think of strength, they usually think of either inner or outer strength. But all strength stems from within. No athlete, celebrity, entrepreneur, or any living person would be as strong as they are without their inner discipline, will, determination and inner strength to overcome challenges.

Life throws us unexpected twists and turns. You may think that we primarily need strength during times of struggle, but we also need it when things are going great. You need to be able to draw upon your inner strength at all times. You will need it to create change, keep going or to walk away.

HAVE STRENGTH WHEN THINGS ARE FALLING APART

When everything seems to be going wrong in your life, it can really start to take a toll on you. The weaker you become, the harder it will be to find your strength. You can find it by thinking of any motivating factor, like a person you do not want to let down. Find something or someone that motivates you to keep going and build momentum on that. You will notice an increase in strength. When your life is falling apart, this allows for the opportunity to rebuild yourself and your life. After going through this process many times, I have learned to trust that this is all happening for your higher good. I now look forward to the new and better things that lie ahead.

PEOPLE WILL EXPECT YOU TO FALL APART

If you have been really struggling, people would understand if you *did* fall apart. They will be amazed by your strength when you keep it together and stay strong. Also, the people who do not believe in you or are not out for your best interests, will expect you to unravel. This in itself, should give you the strength and determination to keep going. I know it does for me.

FIND YOUR STRENGTH TO WALK AWAY

We accept what we think we deserve. When you become stronger, your self-worth begins to hold more value. You will find that you are no longer willing to accept things that you once did, when you were in a different space in your life. The great poet, Maya Angelou always said, "When you know better, you do better." Find the strength to walk away from anything or anyone that diminishes your worth. You deserve better than that!

I wrote a magazine article for a digital magazine. In it I share a true story, which demonstrates me practicing what I preached above:

> From as far back as I can remember, I never felt good enough for my father. The first disappointment I caused for him, was when I was born and failed to come out a boy. I was a born failure and I was constantly reminded of that. It all went downhill from there. But out of everything, the insults were the most damaging to me.
>
> Needless to say I grew up with a distorted sense of self and very low self-esteem. My father moved to another country, the year I became a teenager. *I slowly began to gain inner strength, as I became more spiritual and aware.* I would continue to try and build myself up, but one brief annual visit was enough for me to regress back. I have put myself in this same situation countless times. I would agree to meet my father, get insulted and leave feeling horrible. *Nothing ever changed.* I guess each time I kept hoping it would.
>
> When he called the last time to meet, it sounded different and important. *It would have to sound intriguing if it was going to lure me in again.* We were to meet outside of a landmark hotel, go for a nice walk along the lakeshore and then get a bite to eat. It

sounded nice. I was finally in a good space; living my life authentically. *I have grown and evolved.* Maybe my father has also awakened and lives his life the same way? *Maybe he has changed?!*

The beautiful hot sun was beaming on me as I was driving to meet my father. I was looking forward to our walk along the water. I was 20 minutes early and I started to become anxious and unsettled. I took many deep breaths reminding myself to *stay positive* and *stay in the present moment*. Our past was not the greatest, so in order for us to progress forward, we would need to start from the now.

My father came right on time. It is weird, because every time I see him, he is like a stranger to me. I have never felt close to him, but have often felt obligated to see him because of our blood ties. He first wanted to sit and talk inside the hotel before going out for our sunny walk. *For the first hour,* we were both in the moment and we actually deeply connected. It was nice. We were both adults. *We were equal and I felt the oneness.* For a moment, there was a glimmer of light on our seemingly hopeless father-daughter relationship.

Then the switch started to happen and the energy immediately shifted. My father brought up the past, as if to rub salt in old wounds. *It did not work this time and did not affect me in the least.* So he tried a different tactic to get under my skin. Insults.

The verbal attacks on me and my deceased mother would once be a sure bet to hitting a nerve. Not this time. *For the entire two hours of this, I stayed strong.* I used my truth and love to defend against these unwarranted, vengeful words.

When my father realized that his old ways no longer were going to knock me down, he said:

"*You're strong. When did you get so strong? Way to go!*" and immediately gave me a high-five, as if to congratulate me.

What? Was this a test? Was it just another one of his twisted games? Regardless, there was some sort of peace in conquering my father's approval.

So now that I passed his test and refused to weaken, I guess we can move forward. Maybe now we can finally go for a peaceful walk along the lake? It didn't take long before the insults started again though. This time he kept calling me *weak*. That did not make any sense. I reminded him how he was impressed by my strength and he called me strong, just a few minutes ago. He continued to hammer away the same phase repeatedly...

NOTE TO SELF: EMPOWERMENT

"You are WEAK!"

At that moment, something very strange happened.

I felt as though I was abruptly lifted off the bench to a standing position. I do not know where this strong force came from. I have since been wondering if it had been angels or some kind of divine force lifting me up as if to tell me *I had enough of this and deserve better.*

I said a few quick words to my father, and did not wait for a response. I was out of there so quickly. I had no clue where I was going, but I couldn't walk fast enough.

All this seemed to happen simultaneously without any thought. It was automatic, although this behavior of mine was all new to me. I have never just walked away and left someone, without some kind of warning.

I was relieved to find an exit. I walked outside and was immediately embraced by the warm sun that had been waiting for me lovingly. The further I got from the hotel, the lighter I felt.

I left with a greater appreciation for the new life I have created filled with loving and positive people. I was blessed with the gift of contrast when visiting my father, which truly measured my spiritual and emotional growth.

Everything shifted that afternoon. I was fully healed and full of power. I stayed true to myself. I know that **"I am good enough"**. I have passed the final test. *I left sending love to my father...but most importantly, I left loving myself.*

It has been over two years since I walked away from my father. Not all stories have the happy ending. My father never called to check up on me and ask why I took off so abruptly. He never apologized for treating me poorly. That was it, just like that! I always felt like he did not truly care about me. His actions and words repeatedly showed me throughout my lifetime, but I refused to believe it. I was in denial for all of these years.

The mistake I made, was thinking that when you are a parent you automatically care for your child. Not everyone thinks the same way I do. I do not know what the future holds, as I learned to never say never. At this point, I am happy with the way things are. I no longer have to listen to someone put me down, when they are supposed to love me. I also do not have to wonder if there is ever a chance to mend our relationship. I have closure in knowing that it will most likely not happen.

9

STEP 7: LIVE IN THE MOMENT

Not everything has a happy ending and turns out the way we had hoped, but somehow things always work out even better. When you have tried every solution and things are still not working out for you…just surrender and let be. There is a bigger and better plan that is trying to make its way into your life. Our greatest lessons are learned during our deepest pain. I used to take it personally when others treated me poorly, or were not happy with anything going right in my life. Then I realized that the truly happy people want others to feel the same way and they want to see you succeed.

The people who hurt you and cause you pain, are often deeply hurting inside. That does not make their behavior right. It helps you to see beyond the emotions and to not take what they say or do personally. You may remind them of someone and they may be transferring that hurt onto you. You may be like the person they once were like, or aspire to be, so they may have bitterness towards you for that. Either way, it is not personal. They need to deal with their own issues. They need to heal their own pain, so they are able to love with an open heart. They will continue to hurt others until they heal themselves. When you understand that each person is doing the best they can, at the level they are at, you will have more compassion.

Other people's opinions of you do not matter. You do not have to prove anything to anyone. Not everyone will understand you and not everyone will like you. Accepting this will cause a lot less worry and pain. You will be able to enjoy your life. It is amazing to know that you do not have to settle for a life you are not happy with. There is no reason to hold on to the things that are no longer serving you. You do not have to tolerate people who are not treating you properly. It feels great to take control of your life. To live each day, knowing that you have the choice to remove yourself from any situation that is not serving your higher good. It does not get any more empowering than that!

*****

We have reached the final step. If you took the time to do all the work, then from here on out it is smooth sailing. Now we get to enjoy the moment. How much better can it get? The past is behind us so it is already easier. We are surrounded by loving and encouraging people. We have built ourselves up. Now all you need to focus on is cherishing the moment, and then your life really starts to happen.

CHERISH YOUR LOVED ONES

Live in the moment with your loved ones. Make sure you schedule some time to see them. Engage fully in the conversation and get caught up with every single little thing that is happening. Ultimately we all just want to be loved, heard, seen, valued and appreciated. Life passes by quickly, so do not miss a precious moment.

LIVE IN THE MOMENT AND SEE THINGS AS THEY REALLY ARE

When you live in the moment, you are dealing with the reality as it is placed in front of you. You are able to make better conscious decisions. Your mind is clearer, so you can be more focused and really listen. Do not waste this present moment thinking about the pains of the past or the worries of the future. This only creates more hurt and anxiety. Instead choose uplifting thoughts and be with people who make you feel good. This will turn all of your days around. If you are taking care of the present moment, your future will naturally fall into place.

SAY WHAT YOU WANT TO SAY

If you feel like saying something to someone...say it! Do not hold back. Being authentic and vulnerable humanizes you. You become more approachable and you will have deeper relationships. You do not want to leave anything left unsaid. You never know if you will ever have that opportunity again. In the moment you are putting your full attention and full focus on the person in front of you. Your relationships with your spouse, children, friends, and everyone else gets better because they will feel validated.

Often times the amazing people in your life, get pushed to the back by the demanding and selfish people trying to monopolize all of your time. Make sure the kind, compassionate and unconditionally loving people get moved back up to the forefront of your life.

DO WHAT YOU WANT IN THE MOMENT

If you get the urge or desire to do something...do it! Do not wait. Embrace the opportunity that is being offered to you, as it is happening. If something is extremely important to you, then now is the right time to start. You may never accomplish those amazing things if you are always waiting for the perfect time to be ready. You will never have to wonder, what if...

Live in the moment and you will minimize guilt, regrets, and missed opportunities. Realizing that we only have to focus on the moment, eliminates a lot of needless stress right there. A lot of our stress is just in our head. You will be less anxious because you are slowing your life down and you will not be overwhelmed. You will cherish people and all that life has to offer you. Your life will be enriched and fulfilling. It is important that you embrace each moment because without warning, your life can change in an instant.

In the moment you also notice the beauties of life and you will become even more grateful. You will pay more attention to the birds, the sun, the water and your surroundings. You may notice things that were there all along, but you just walked by them. These are the simple things in life, but they are the beautiful moments. Now that you have completed the 7 steps, you no longer have the same stresses and can enjoy the moment. Because you are paying attention, you will notice when you are making the wrong choices or when things do not feel right so you can stop things immediately. You can change directions and make better choices before it is too difficult to steer around. The way you felt in the past, may not be how you feel today. Re-evaluate your life often so you can make changes before veering too far off course.

WHAT WE FOCUS ON EXPANDS

You build up energy and momentum towards the things you focus on. If you want something in your life to continue to expand, then focus on it. As far as I am concerned, if you are taking a risk on yourself, it is not a risk. So, expand yourself. Live beyond your walls, fears, and comfort zones. Only you know what is best for you. It feels exhilarating to push through your comfort zone and challenge yourself. You will never know what you are capable of, until you try.

If you live in the moment, you become more aware. Time slows down so you are able to think more clearly and make better decisions. Do not allow anyone to pressure you. When you get used to being in the moment, you will be more sensitive to this pressure and you will begin to feel uneasy. When you start to feel this, stop it right away and take a deep breath. Tell the person you need time to think about it or sleep on it. This will prevent you from making mistakes that you will regret later.

ASKING FOR HELP

Allow people to treat you how you would treat them. Give them the same opportunity to have that amazing feeling you have when you give or help someone. It feels great to receive the love and respect you deserve. Ask for help when you need it, instead of waiting until it is too late. I could have asked some of my friends for help, but I had too much pride. I did not want to admit that things were going wrong. As a result, they could not help me because too much damage was already done.

If you are independent and self-sufficient, then asking for help can be the hardest thing in the world. You are the one who people always count on. You are strong and can do everything on your own. You feel like you do not need help. Even if you are doing things the hard way, you are happy because you are proving to yourself and everyone around that you can do it on your own. If you are like this then it can be extremely difficult to admit when you need help. It may be unfathomable to ask for help and to accept it.

ADMITTING YOU NEED HELP

You can be in denial for a long time because it is hard to admit to yourself that you need help. It is even harder to admit to others, especially if you have created a pattern of doing every single thing on your own. You cannot tell them that you now are the one needing help? You may feel like a failure and you may be afraid of being a burden. You do not want to bother anyone. You are a positive person and do not want to bring anyone down. It is impossible to go through life doing everything on your own. It is much harder and not very much fun. Asking for help, eases the burden.

If you need or want help, then ask for it in the moment. Do not wait until it is too late and becomes an even bigger problem. Be vulnerable. Are you worried that people will think that you are not as strong as you appear to be? You do not think that of others when they ask you to help them, so why is it any different when you need them to help you? It takes great strength and courage to ask for help! Let people see the true you so they can be there for you. Show them that you are human and have feelings, struggles, and fears, just like everyone else. You do not have to pretend that you are Superman/woman. Be authentic. Be free to be yourself and allow others to really get to know you. The right people will love you even more for this.

You will learn a valuable lesson when you ask for help. You will find out which family members and friends will be there for you. People who truly care about you, want to help you. They want to see you happy. They want to ease your struggles.

ACCEPTING AND RECEIVING HELP

This is the hardest part, especially if you are the one always used to helping or giving. To be on the receiving end, may seem foreign and unsettling. It can also be very humbling. Yes you are able to do it yourself, and you have proven it many times over. There is nothing wrong with accepting help. Why is it acceptable when you are always there for people, but you have problems receiving help for yourself? You know that joy you feel when you have helped make a difference in someone's life? When you have helped lift a great burden? Why are you depriving other people from doing the same for you and having the same feeling?

It is not all give, give, give or take, take, take. These relationships are one-sided. If you only give without receiving, then you will find yourself attracting mainly "Takers". This works for a while, since it fulfills your desire to give, help, and please. Quite often though, these "Takers" only take. When you need them, they are not there. When you no longer give, they will move on to someone else. There should be a healthy balance of giving and receiving. It is a feeling that both of you are there for one another in a time of need. There is a mutual respect and appreciation, without taking each other for granted. Your life becomes easier and happier because you become a team and work together.

Who would have ever thought that it was this simple? There is nothing wrong with balancing your life. It requires undoing years of internal programming and changing the way you think. Healthy relationships are two-sided. By asking for help, you will find out much more quickly, who are the ones you can count on and are there for you. Whether it is for support, assistance, guidance or advice, let people help you. Your life will be easier and happier. Your relationships will be much deeper and more authentic. You are not thinking badly of the people you are helping, so let others feel that same joy. Your life does not have to be such a struggle.

IT'S NOT ME, IT'S YOU

Why do we take things so personally? We are the first ones to turn the blame onto us. If someone is angry, we wonder what *we* did. Also, if we have not heard from someone for some time, we may automatically think that we did something wrong. Somehow, we take things too personally.

If you are surrounded by someone who is always criticizing you, take a moment to re-evaluate. Bullies and manipulative people commonly use the same tactic. They blame you and criticize you, and before you know it, somehow you are the one apologizing. Also, look how they talk to and treat others. You may be surprised to find out that you are not the only one they treat poorly. No matter what you do, it will not be good enough and you will still be criticized. Do not take any of what they are doing or saying personally. This is one of the best revelations.

LET GO OF SOME CONTROL AND LET BE

Having complete control was an extremely stressful way to live my life. I hated the "not knowing" and I hated surprises. I needed to be in control of everything. That way things would not go wrong, my life would run more smoothly and I would not get hurt. I knew what to expect and I thought that being in control would ensure a better outcome. I would analyze every person and situation that entered my life. I had to make sense of everything. I had to try and figure out and understand, so that no one would pull a fast one on me. I was not going to play the part of a fool again. Trying to control everything was the only way I thought I could stop this.

The people who tend to do this are the ones who have been hurt many times in the past. Your guard is up, and your wall is up so high that no one can break through. Do you hate not knowing the outcome of things? Do you feel like you need to make sense of everything? Sometimes the things that happen, do not make sense. Often people do not make sense. Trying to make sense of everything can be exhausting and a waste of time. Sometimes just letting things be and not trying to understand it, is the best way.

MAKE THINGS RIGHT

If we did someone wrong, either intentionally or unintentionally, we have a chance to make it right. Own up to your mistakes and don't be afraid to express how you feel. Apologize to the person you have hurt. Sometimes that is all it takes to make things right. If by chance the person is unable to forgive or forget, honor that and release it. You have done the best you could. All you can do is continue to make better choices and treat people better moving forward. Hopefully, one day they will come around and see that you are a changed person. If not, your life will be better with your healthier choices and attitude.

MISSED OPPORTUNITY

If you let something pass you by, do not dwell over it and allow it to prevent you from moving forward. You have two choices. You can chase after it, or welcome a new door to open and not let that opportunity slip by you.

BE PROACTIVE

Know who/what is important to you. If you spend time nurturing your relationships with those people, you will always be happy. Do not be afraid to tell them that you love them, as it can never be too many times. Do the things that you have always wanted to do and say.

MAKE LESS TIME FOR THE UNWORTHY PEOPLE

When I rearranged my priorities and made more time for the ones who mattered most, and less time for the ones who always "needed" me, the strangest thing happened. One by one...they disappear out of my life. When they were not getting all that they wanted from me, they moved on to the next person. Do not be surprised if the same thing happens to you.

MAKE TIME TO DO THE THINGS YOU LOVE

It is important to make time to do things you love. Life cannot be all work and no play. Schedule time for activities that bring you joy or enhance your life.

DOES THE PAST KEEP CREEPING IN?

The past can keep creeping in, even if you are consciously trying to move forward and want to forget about it. It is hard to let go of the past because it is all that you have ever known up until this very moment. It can feel familiar to you and somewhat comfortable.

The residual effects of the past can cause anxiety. You may worry that you are going to make the same mistakes and bad choices. When someone/something triggers that emotional response, it can remind you of your "old" way of life. Also, the people you are trying to remove yourself from, have a wonderful way of squirming their way back in. They know just the right things to say and do to reel you back in...but they never change, do they? They have this incredible sense that you are moving towards great things and a better life. They are making their last desperate attempts at keeping you stuck. The guilt and manipulation have some sort of hold on you. You can become disappointed when you allow the old garbage from the past back into your life. You may feel as though you are regressing, but this is all part of the process. Hang in there!

USE THE PAST TO RECOGNIZE CONTRAST

When you have been used by negative people, you will find the opposite to be refreshing. You would not be able to recognize or value amazing qualities in a good person, if you were not shown the contrast. Embrace people who are positive and add value to your life. You deserve this.

Past lessons and people reintroduce themselves into your life, to give you a chance to measure your growth.

USE THE PAST TO BECOME MORE GRATEFUL

The past will help you to become more grateful. When you are around people who are encouraging, nurturing, and loving, you will cherish them more. You will be grateful that you made better choices that enhance your life.

EMBRACE POSITIVE CHANGES

It takes time to adjust to your improved life. Do not wreck anything good that enters your life. If you are used to struggle, it can seem "too good to be true". Do not transfer what someone else has done to you in the past, onto an innocent person. Until proven otherwise, enjoy and welcome all positive things. The past helps you to learn and grow. This is where you have gained your strength. This is where you have learned your most valuable lessons. You have the power to not allow the past to control you. Allow yourself to let go and adjust to all your new and positive changes. Keep pushing forward...you have made it this far!

OVERCOMING FEAR

Fear can paralyze you and your life can become stuck. We were not born with fear. As children, we were born carefree. There was no such thing as the fear of failure, success, death, love or the unknown. Think about it. You may need to return back to your earliest memories to remember this time. You may even have to use your imagination, but there once was a time when we had no fear of trying new things. At such a young age, you seemed invincible. Falling down, or getting hurt did not stop you from learning how to walk or run. Making mistakes or mispronouncing words did not prevent you from learning how to talk. We were not afraid to go up to other children in the playground or beach and instantly become friends. We were loving and open to everyone, even if it was not reciprocated. When first introduced to fear, we faced it dead on and overcame it very quickly. By the time we got to the age of learning how to ride a bike, we had fallen many times and may have developed a fear of falling. That still did not stop us. We were indestructible, and then things changed.

As the years went by, negative experiences, circumstances and people all contributed to our fears. When a fear is instilled in our mind, it becomes a block. The more time we spend not facing our fears, the more control and hindrance it will have on our lives. Now that we have acknowledged the root of our fears and how they have developed, we can take the time to conquer them.

FALLING IN LOVE AGAIN

Being vulnerable and trusting again is extremely difficult. Trust me, I know this firsthand and all too well. It is scary to open up your heart after being hurt or betrayed. The main person you need to trust and love, is yourself. Once you have reached that point, you are ready to take the risk and love again. *If you are providing honesty, respect, love, compassion and kindness in a relationship…do not feel bad for wanting the same in return.*

BEING JUDGED

The more you overcome your fears and live your life "outside the box", the more people will judge you. Mainly, it is because they do not have the courage to do what you are doing. You cannot please everyone. People who truly care about you will encourage your exciting life and bold risks. The most important thing is to do what makes you happy.

The things you are fearful of are never as scary as they appear in your mind. After you conquer your fear, you will wander why you were afraid in the first place. Do not waste another minute. Your life is waiting for you on the other side of fear.

WASTING YOUR BREATH

Do not waste your breath trying to prove or explain yourself to people who are not out for your best interests and refuse to believe you. I have been through this enough times to know that you are fighting a losing battle. There is nothing you can say or do that will convince these types of people. The people who truly know you, value the amazing person you are. The truth and your character speak for itself, so you do not need to say a word.

WASTING YOUR TIME

We all have the same 24 hours in a day. Picture how you would like your life to look like. Are you focusing on things that do not matter in the "big picture"? Make sure you are doing things today that bring you happiness, fulfillment and closer to your goal. Is what you are doing benefiting others or yourself? Are you wasting your time with the wrong people or ones who are treating you poorly? Is there someone else more worthy of your time who you may be neglecting?

WASTING YOUR ENERGY

Are you wasting your energy trying to help someone who doesn't want to be helped? Maybe you think they need help, but they do not believe they do. You can spend a lot of time and energy and get nowhere. They can be in the same predicament years later. Often they don't even appreciate it. When people are ready for your help, they will ask you. Or you can tell by their efforts in trying to better themselves and their situation. Also, do not feel guilty if you need to relax. There is nothing wrong with taking time to refresh, regroup and regain your energy.

BACK TO LIVING IN THE MOMENT

It is not as important how people were in the past, as it is who they are today. If a person has changed or has grown from a past experience or relationship, enjoy *that* person. How are people treating you right now? How are you feeling right now? What is the situation right now? This moment is all we have control of. We cannot change or erase the past and nothing is guaranteed in the future.

Your present moment is a residual effect of all your past choices. If you want to change your future, you are going to have to make different choices and take different actions. Pay attention to your feelings. What makes you happy? What makes you sad? Angry? Overwhelmed? These feelings help to filter out what you do want, from what you do not want. If you are feeling negative, then you are out of alignment with who you truly are. Let your feelings be your guide. Pay attention to the direction you are being pushed towards. The things people keep saying to you and the opportunities that continue to present themselves to you, may all be pointing you towards your destiny.

I have learned that life is so much easier when you are in alignment with who you truly are. I was making it more difficult than it had to be. Your life is not meant to be so hard, it is meant to be fun and easy. Everything unfolds in divine order. Trust God's plan for you, it may actually be better than yours.

10

YOU GOT THIS!

You are over the hump and the hardest part is over. We have covered a lot. It will take some time to really go through, absorb and implement these 7 steps. These steps rectified a lot of the damage in my life. It brought me back to my true self and what I was born here to do. I made it simpler for you, so it will take you way less time, and you will not have to learn the hard way like I did. You have all the tools you need and you also have the desire to improve your life. Otherwise you would not be reading this book. You now understand what is not working for you and how to change it. You have done all this inner work and you never have to go back to that place again. It is only maintenance and moving forward from here.

*****

NOTE TO SELF: EMPOWERMENT

My entire life has transformed. My whole new world is filled with positive, happy, supportive, encouraging and loving people. Was this world here all along? Was I so far off course that it was impossible to catch a glimpse of it in the far distance? I am grateful that I found it. I feel safe and protected, when before I was continually guarded and sheltered. I feel free, instead of like a prisoner and a victim. I can honestly say, I have very minimal stress in my life. There is an unwavering sense of inner peace combined with inner strength. Almost everything on my vision board has come into fruition. I believe the few things that haven't are on its way soon.

I could not be happier. It feels great to be sure of who I truly am and the direction I am going. My internal guidance system never steers me wrong. I am strong enough to help inspire, uplift and empower. I feel incredibly blessed to live out my life's purpose. I am now married to the man of my dreams, who loves me unconditionally. He helped me to open my heart up fully and is also an amazing father figure to my two girls.

I am enjoying life more than ever and I could never go back to the way my life used to be. I know better. I am extremely selective with whom I allow in my close circle. My life is as congruent on the outside as it is on the inside, and I am no longer suffering silently. In fact, I am no longer suffering at all. It seems surreal how easy and joyous my life is. I have no more drama and I no longer have to worry about the ones closest to me hurting me the most.

My sister Stacy and I are in a great place in our lives. I also have the power in knowing that if things ever change,

I can always make different choices. People make mistakes. We are all human. At some point, you have to let it go.

I feel we needed to go through all that we did in order to have a deeper understanding of each other. Our small family only gets together a few times a year, but there is always love and laughter. Things are good because I keep quiet and I do not mention the past. I have now reached a crossroad. I know serving others is my purpose, and I must speak the truth in order to do this. Sharing my story and the pivotal moments are essential components for me to help guide, motivate, inspire, and uplift you through your hardships.

I have not spoken or heard from my father in over two years. The day I walked away from him, I left the hurtful things behind and chose to only focus on the good memories of my father. He always had really funny jokes and phrases. I often find myself repeating his jokes to my husband. In fact, I said one of his silly phrases this morning. It is great that I can enjoy this part of him from afar and I no longer have to worry about getting verbally knocked down. Find your purpose and your power within, and do not let anyone tear you down. No one can ever take away your power and happiness without your permission.

Every single aspect of my life is extraordinary. I could not ask for a better husband, children, friends, family or career. I actually feel like I am bragging when I talk about my life now and I do not want to do that. I merely want to point out the contrast from how my life used to be like and now. Currently, I am living my dream. Once you get here, there is no turning back. Life keeps getting better and all from the inner work I did with these 7 steps. This is when I discovered my true self and unstoppable power within. I now feel that I have enough strength to carry the entire universe. I really hope that you take the time to thoroughly do the steps, so you can experience the full extent of how great life feels.

On a spiritual level, the people who have hurt you the most end up being your greatest teachers. For that matter, I do not take anything personally. I have no hard feelings towards anyone who has hurt me because they taught me the lessons I needed in order to live my purpose. I would not be able to learn how to find my inner strength if I did not have people in my life who were constantly trying to take it away. I also needed to have people in my life who would put me down, so I could learn how to believe in myself and find out who I truly was.

I have known since the age of ten that I was going to write a book. If I was going to learn my purpose, each person in my life needed to play their role in order to teach me. If I was going to learn inner strength and self-love, I would need to get hurt a lot. As a result, I have unwavering inner strength to uplift, inspire and help you. After helping many people, I found that I connected with them through sharing my story. I have a deeper sense of compassion because of all I went through and I have a strong sense of purpose. It was important to turn my wounds into wisdom so I could use it to help you. We all have our own stories. Maybe one day you will share your story and help others. It takes courage to stay true to who you are. Now that you did the inner work, we can focus on your life purpose.

WHY ARE WE HERE?

Purpose and passion are the same thing. What is your passion? I believe everyone was born with a purpose. The tricky part is figuring out what that purpose is. At some point in your life, you will wonder about the meaning of your life, your mission or your calling. You may start to question if you are meant to do something more with your life or if there is something greater than what is going on presently. It may require a lot of soul-searching. The sooner you recognize your higher purpose, the faster you can live your most successful and fulfilling life.

ASK A PARENT OR SOMEONE WHO KNOWS YOU BEST WHAT YOUR PURPOSE IS

Ever since my daughter Brooklyn was young, she has been entertaining. She has an incredible passion for singing, dancing and music. Brooklyn was extremely shy and soft-spoken throughout most of her childhood. Most people would never have imagined that she would have the confidence to go up and sing in public. As her mother, I could see her deepest passion. I would consciously make efforts to encourage her and to help her overcome her biggest fears, in order to fuel this inner driving force.

She spends the majority of her time teaching herself how to play instruments, singing and writing songs. Often, I go into her room and remind her that she needs to go to sleep because it is getting really late and she has to wake up early. She waits just long enough for me to go to bed. As I lay in bed, I can hear Brooklyn singing and playing guitar or piano. That kid never stops, and I never stop her. For one, she sounds amazing. Most importantly, how can I interfere with someone so passionate about doing what she loves? It is clear what her passion, purpose and drive is in life, and I do not want to be the one responsible for getting in the way of that.

Not everyone is blessed with such encouragement. People can be mean. You could have had a parent or someone close to you, continually put you down and discourage you. If you grew up this way, more than likely this would become very damaging to your self-esteem and carry on into adulthood. With each passing day, your passion in life begins to dwindle and you can begin to hide your true self. Many of us were forced to please our parents. Maybe you were not allowed to fully be who you were meant to be. You may have fallen down the wrong path. You may feel as though there couldn't possibly be a purpose to your life.

I forgot how creative I was! That side of me got buried somehow. I thought I was really analytical because I would always analyze things as a form of protecting myself. Because I was hurt and fooled so many times, I analyzed in order to be a step ahead of those trying to pull the wool over my eyes. Working through these processes got me back to where and who I was meant to be, and what I was born to do.

"Maybe the journey isn't so much about becoming anything. Maybe it's about unbecoming everything that really isn't you so you can be who you were meant to be in the first place."

-Author Unknown

THINK BACK TO WHEN YOU WERE A CHILD

What did you love doing? What were you naturally good at? You were so good at it that you almost took it for granted. It was so simple that you did not even think it is that big of a deal. You will discover that your talents and purpose have been with you since as long as you can remember. We often lose sight of this as we get older.

When you are doing what you love and being who you are truly meant to be, it fuels you. It excites you and energizes you to the point where you can do that thing for hours. You lose track of time. This is your calling. This is your purpose. Why hold that back from you and the rest of the world? Your calling will never go away. It will continue to silently nudge at you. If you trust in your God-given talent and passion and use it to help people, your life will unfold in unimaginable ways.

DREAM BIG AND LIVE YOUR BEST LIFE

Dream BIG. You hear this all the time, but are you following your dreams? Are you taking action, or is your dream just burning away inside of you? The exciting part begins the moment you take that first step towards making your dreams become a reality. Sure it can be scary. It may seem risky to go outside of your comfort zone and the comfort zone of those around you. It often involves making changes, taking risks, hard work and big sacrifices. Not many people are comfortable or ready for that.

Some of you have already pursued your dreams and have accomplished great things. Many of you are in the process of accomplishing your goals. It takes a lot of courage and determination to do this, but it is well worth it. Do not make the mistake of many others and give up too early. How much does your dream mean to you? So many people or excuses can get in the way. If your dream is important enough to you, then you will find a way to make it come true. You will stop at nothing.

PEOPLE MAY NOT UNDERSTAND YOUR DREAM

All that matters is that your dream makes sense to you and that you wholeheartedly believe in it. No one will understand your dream better than you. Do you think anyone understood the Wright Brothers' vision of inventing the airplane? It didn't seem possible did it? The list of fascinating inventions and accomplishments that people didn't understand or thought were possible are endless. You are no different. You can accomplish great things. Not everyone is going to understand this big dream you have in your head. Hold on tight to your vision and take steps to make it become your reality. People will eventually comprehend what you have always known deep down inside. You need to make it happen and show it to them.

PEOPLE MAY TRY TO DISCOURAGE YOU

People may say your dream is crazy. Some people, who are uncomfortable with change may try and persuade you to keep living your life exactly how it is now - the safe and comfortable way. What if you are not happy? What if you feel like you are meant to do something "more"? This is your life and you need to do what is best for you. You need to live your life the way you see it. You do not want to look back on your life, regretting not taking that chance on pursuing your dream.

PEOPLE MAY START TO HATE YOU OR BECOME JEALOUS

As you get closer to accomplishing your dream, people may start to get in the way of it. They may become envious and start creating obstacles for you. They may become jealous because they are not happy. They see you starting to create great things and change your life around. This can stir up some jealousy and hate within themselves for not taking the risks like you are. Do not take this to heart. I often take this as a compliment and a guide to how close I am to achieving my goal. Stay strong.

YOU MAY START TO DOUBT YOUR DREAM

You may start to doubt your dream if you are not seeing results right away. The obstacles and hard work can become challenging at times. You may start to question if it is worth it, or start to wonder if you made the right decision. In order to accomplish your dreams, you cannot be your own worst enemy. It is important to not limit yourself and your potential. Believe in yourself and you will accomplish great things.

It is your dream. How important it is to you will determine the actions that you are willing to take. If you believe that you can do it, then you most definitely can. Show others that you can make the impossible, possible. Most importantly, prove to yourself that you can do it. It is never too late to live your dream.

If you are not sure what it is, then think about what you are the most passionate about. What are you naturally good at? What are people asking you to help with? It could be advice, fixing computers, writing, singing...the list is endless. There are so many people in the world waiting for you to share your gifts. There are countless people you can help.

You are so sure of yourself and confident because you now know your true self. You know what works and what does not. You are not going to compromise your beliefs or who you are. Your inner voice becomes stronger and your purpose becomes clearer. Once that inner voice and your inner knowing have more power than anything else going on externally, you will have mastered your life. When you get to this point, you will find that you cannot do anything else except your purpose. It will keep nagging at you until you actually do it. It is a calling that will keep getting stronger and louder.

Waiting for the right moment may never happen. Waiting can easily turn moments into years. You do not want to look back at all the time you have wasted. Maybe you already feel like you have wasted enough time and you are desperate for a change. Often when we are waiting around, we take for granted that people and opportunities will always be there for us. We also think and hope that things will change on their own, eventually. You will feel better if you stop waiting and start doing the things you want to do and love. People become comfortable with their lives. Sometimes things happen to free up time so you are able to pursue your dreams and passions.

The Universe has got your back. Doors will open and close to help direct you to where you need to be. There are no accidents and no coincidences. You are exactly where you are supposed to be. Each moment is preparing you for your grander plan. Whatever happens to you that may seem to go against your will, is really pushing you towards a better direction and forcing you to adjust your choices. You deserve better, and it is on its way.

You are extremely valuable to this world. Even if you do not feel it at times, you make a difference. You may never truly feel ready and there will always be some sort of obstacle in the way. I am here to tell you that you are ready now! You do not have to be perfect, you just need to get started. You can improve things as you go along. The most important thing is that you take that brave, first step. You are loved whether you feel worthy of it or not. Do not undervalue your worth and contribution to others.

NOTE TO SELF: EMPOWERMENT

People need the best version of you. Do not deprive the world from your unique gifts and talents. Only you can live out your dream and purpose. There is no competition.

I truly care about your well-being and I hope I positively impacted your life. I am here for you beyond this book. Please do not ever hesitate to reach out to me at: trina@trinahall.com.

ABOUT THE AUTHOR

Trina Hall is an author, blogger, speaker and life coach. She has published articles in the Australian digital magazine, *ONE mag*. Trina has had a tumultuous life, and has gotten knocked down repeatedly until she reached rock bottom. As a result, she has gained decades of incredible wisdom and insight. There is no beating life experience when it comes to learning and teaching.

In addition, she has traveled to learn from several of the top leaders in the personal development industry. Trina's balance of vulnerability, compassion and unwavering strength helps inspire, guide and empower countless people across the globe. Whether it be through her writings or in person, she has an innate gift to lessen suffering and transform lives.

Trina lives in Cambridge, Ontario, Canada with her husband and two daughters. She grew up in Northern Ontario and is a Southern California girl at heart.

Find out more about Trina at: www.trinahall.com

www.ingramcontent.com/pod-product-compliance
Lightning Source LLC
Chambersburg PA
CBHW051649040426
42446CB00009B/1053